Anonymous

Wotton-Under-Edge

What to see and how to see it with original sketches, also, a description of

the neighbourhood

Anonymous

Wotton-Under-Edge
What to see and how to see it with original sketches, also, a description of the neighbourhood

ISBN/EAN: 9783337096854

Printed in Europe, USA, Canada, Australia, Japan

Cover: Foto ©ninafisch / pixelio.de

More available books at **www.hansebooks.com**

WOTTON-UNDER-EDGE,

What to see and how to see it

WITH ORIGINAL SKETCHES,

ALSO A

Description of the Neighbourhood.

2ND EDITION, ENLARGED.

COMPILED BY
MARGARET AND ISABELLA TAIT.

Printed by Herrick & Gorham, Tolsey Works, Wotton-under-Edge.

1897.

PREFACE.

THE object of this little book is to supply a want long felt in the neighbourhood; to connect the ages past, with the one now passing, and to enable those unacquainted with the district to gain some slight knowledge of its beauty and interest. The Geologist, the Botanist, the Archæologist and the admirers of beautiful scenery will find in Wotton-under-Edge and locality much to gratify their various pursuits and tastes.

WOTTON-UNDER-EDGE

YE TOWNE CRIER.

HIS Parish lies in the Hundred of Berkeley, four miles south from Dursley, two and a half east from Charfield, and nineteen south from Gloucester. (Before the time of King Alfred some parts of England were divided into counties; each county was divided into districts called *Hundreds*, either from the number of families or Landed Proprietors in each: these Hundreds were divided again into Tithings). Wotton-under-Edge is situated on a pleasant eminence, part of the Cotswold Range, which is well wooded. The Cotswold Hills are covered with a thin calcareous sand, derived from the oolite rocks on which they rest; some parts make good sheep downs; others, when carefully tilled, bear oats and barley. The vale is the chief seat of tillage; the land there is well sheltered, the air mild, the soil rich, and the growth forward. They obtained their double name and meaning from "Coed" in the British language and "Weold" in Saxon, both signifying a *wood*, and together make a kind of tautology. The town of Wotton-under-Edge overlooks to the east a "Combe" or little valley, hence its original name "Wood Town under Ridge;" it commands an extensive and beautiful prospect, especially from the brow of the hill called "West Ridge," from which may be seen the ample and luxuriant vale, richly beset with villages and farmhouses. Beyond, on a clear day, can be seen Lansdown Hill near Bath, Bristol, Sodbury Camp Hill, Hawkesbury Upton Monument, Berkeley Castle, Wickwar, the Severn (the " Sabrina " of the Romans), Dean Forest, and the Welsh mountains. The " Knoll " was crowned with a clump of Scotch fir trees, which were a landmark to all the country between Berkeley and Bath, these were ruthlessly destroyed and made into a bonfire at the time of the celebration of peace after the Crimean War (a fate which had befallen a former group of firs at the Waterloo rejoicings.) The hill is again crowned with trees in commemoration of Queen Victoria's Jubilee; Lord Fitzhardinge planting them and building round a substantial wall for protection against the strong gales which occasionally blow. His Lordship also for a small annual payment granted the town of Wotton the right for a term of twenty one years, to place a number of seats and benches upon the crest of the hill and its approaches; visitors to this delightful height may rest upon the way, admire as they ascend, and enjoy in comfort the beautiful panorama stretched out around them. "In the reign of Queen Elizabeth, the Earl of Leicester with an extraordinary number of attendants, and a multitude of Country people, came to Wotton, and thence to Michaelwood Lodge, casting down part of the pales, which like a little park then enclosed the Lodge, (for the gates were too narrow to let in his train) and from thence to Wotton Hill, where he played a match at Stoball." (Smyth's Manuscript) " Stoball " or Stoolball was a local game resembling Cricket. The following are old proverbs of the Hundred of Berkeley concerning the hill.

When Wotton Hill doth wear a Cap,
Let Horton Towne beware of that.

The foggy mist turns that way into rain—

When West Ridge wood is motley
Then tis time to sowe barley.

The superior healthiness of the Cotswolds is in a great measure due to the dryness of the atmosphere, countries abounding with calcareous matters are seldom visited with epidemic disorders. Azote or Septon is the cause of most epidemics. In calcareous countries the excess of Septon in the air is prevented by its attaching itself to the quicklime of the soil, as fast as it is extricated—in other places it is wafted in the atmosphere and forms various compounds. The Old Town, which stood in the rear of the present one, was destroyed by fire in the reign of King John; the site is still called the "Old Town," and a spot named "The Brands" is commemorative of the fire. On its restoration, in the time of Henry III a charter was granted to Maurice Lord Berkeley, and Johanna de Berkeley, his mother, who held the Manor of Wotton in Jointure, empowering them to hold markets, and a fair, also constituting it a "Borough," the corporate body to consist of a Mayor and Aldermen, the Mayor being chosen at the annual court leet, and after his term of office to become an Alderman, but without magisterial jurisdiction, nor had the Borough power to send a Member to Parliament, it being a "burgh" before the first Parliament was called in 1261. The Market was to be held weekly upon Friday, and the Fair yearly, to last three days, "That is to say, on the vigil, on the day, and on the morrow of the exaltation of the 'Holy Cross,' unless such market and such fair shall be to the prejudice of neighbouring markets and fairs." The hats and cloaks of the Mayor and Aldermen have long since been abandoned, but the dress of the "Town Crier" has lately been resuscitated. Almost the only emblem of office pertaining to the Corporation is a very handsome Mace, with the following inscription:—"EX DONO PRŒHON: AUGUSTI COM: DE BERKELEY, PRO USA MAJORIS BURGI SUI DE WOTTON, A.D. 1747." Upon it are the Royal Arms of England, the Rose of England, the Thistle of Scotland, the Lily of France, the Harp of Ireland, and the arms of the Berkeley family. Flemish weavers came over considerably during the reigns of Henry I. and Stephen—Madox in his History of the Exchequer mentions that cities and towns paid fines to King John that they might buy and sell dyed cloth. A cloth maker in Gloucestershire had the surname of "Webb" given him by King Edward III and there was a privilege granted to the cloth makers settled in this country, that they might weave the cloth any length or breadth suited to their own convenience. Leland, in his "Itinerary," written in the reign of Henry VIII calls Wotton "*A praty Market Towne, welle occupied withe Clothiars, haringe one faire longe Strete, and it stondithe clyringe towards* *the rotes of an hill."* Though Leland takes note of one street only, it is probable there were others in his time. The following names appear in the writings of the next century, viz-High Street, Sow Lane, the Chipping or Market Place, Chipping Lane, Bradley Street, Hawe Street, Church Lane, and Sym Lane (or Seam Lane,) the edge of the Borough. There has been no alteration in the names of the streets, but others have been added, such as "Culverhay" from "Culver,"* a pigeon,

Doore in ye Longe Strete

and Saxon "Hœg,"† a hedge, the pigeon cot being formerly near the church; "The Cloud," from a Welsh word signifying "a bank." "Merlin Haven" or "Merlin's Haven," which more than a hundred years ago was a bleak, woody hill, probably the rest of the "Merlin," a kind of hawk, hence its name "Merlin's Haven"; in the days of Harold no person of rank stirred out without his hawk, a gift of two Norway hawks was considered a welcome present by King John: but the name "Merlin's Haven," may be of Arthurian origin as Arthur had his legendary court in Wales, while Merlin wandered about for forty years among hills in a state of semi madness, 573 A.D. In a deed dated 12th Aug. re *Jacobi* a field called "*Mare Haven*" is mentioned, (Gentleman's Magazine.) "Bear Lane"

* Ogilvie.   † "Hœg" Chaucer.

or "Borough Lane," another edge of the borough; the Chipping, or "Stone Cheping," or "Stoning Cheping," with the market house and the "Greene Cheping" pay a ground rental of £10 yearly. "The Butts" was formerly an archery ground. In the time of Edward IV. every Englishman was ordered to provide himself with a bow of his own height, and butts were directed to be put up in every township, for the inhabitants to shoot at on feast days. What boy does not love to hear of "Robin Hood" and all his exploits; every tree would supply a bow and arrows, the entrails of beasts furnished a string, and thus was procured a rude instrument of destruction, none the less deadly because so simple.

Charles I. had a temporary garrison in Wotton, consisting of a regiment of horse (according to Corbet), who were driven out of the town by the Parliamentary Party under Colonel Massey, and having suffered the loss of six killed, twelve

Ye Towne Stocks & Pillorie

made prisoners the rest escaped to Bristol. It was again garrisoned for the King by eight hundred men, and attacked by Captain Backhouse with two hundred horse and dragoons, the latter being forced to beat a retreat. Coins stamped "Carolus I." are frequently discovered in the town. The one shown in our sketch was found in a garden, and is

A Brass weight for the gold ½ Sov of Charles I as marked $\frac{V}{S}$.

Two godly Martyrs were consumed by fire at Wotton-under-Edge, Gloucestershire, viz- John Horn and a woman. They died in a constant faith, so gloriously did the Lord work in them; that death unto them was life, and life with a blotted conscience was death (Foxe's Book of Martyrs.) A spot in Old Town is pointed out where the martyrdom took place.

Of the Old Town Meeting House no regular History has been kept, but being the oldest Dissenting Church in this town it is highly probable that it originated in the ejectment of the Nonconformist Ministers in 1662, particularly as at that time and previously there was a "godly Society" who were in the habit of assembling together to pray and repeat sermons and sing. To this society the Revd Joseph Woodward, M.A., who was at that time Master of the Free Grammar School at Wotton joined himself when he became subject to serious impressions. (Ancient Manuscript.) The present place of worship was erected between 1701 and 1703 the cottages which stood where the present Chapel now stands were purchased 1701 and the present Chapel was conveyed to Trustees in 1703.

In a "Booke of Accompts" is the following entry, 1660, PAYD THE TRUMPETTERS AT PROCLAYMING THE KINGES MAJESTIE (CHARLES II.) 10s. PAYD TO JAMES BUBB FOR WINE DRANKE AT PROCLAYMING THE KINGES MAJESTIE £5 5s. 0d.

The manufactures were formerly woollen cloth and paper, and the clothing trade was also carried on very extensively, which was introduced by some Flemish weavers, who resided at the "Brands" Old Town; the terraces on the hill at Combe were used by them it is believed for the culture of the vine.

Although the former activity and wealth formed by the industrious cloth weavers have passed away, with the accompanying clack and rattle of looms in the valley of Little Avon, there are still a few Mills left which within the past fifteen years, have gradually developed a special industry, and bid fair to aid in restoring the life once so characteristic of it. The works are Messrs Tubbs & Lewis's, New Mills, between Wotton and Charfield, and their Abbey and Langford Mills, about a mile up the stream; they deal largely in elastic and braids, and having restored the New Mills which had been built about one hundred years, introduced there the manufacture of the pin—over a ton of pins are produced per week: both steam and water power are used, and very interesting it is to watch the progress of a pin from a piece of straight wire, to the pin sticking in the papers: no telephone could venture within the precincts of the machine room of the pin factory, the noise of the action of a score or two of pin machines each turning out its two hundred per minute is deafening.

The Wotton Town Hall is built upon the foundation of the former Market House, which stood in the "Stone Cheping" or "Stoning Cheping" close by the plot called the "Greene Cheping" where is held the yearly Fair—but the weekly market is now transferred to Charfield fortnightly cattle sale; the Townhall until lately was supported with pillars of stonework leaving open space between, where the weekly market was held, now some good rooms occupy this space, viz:- Reading room and Free Library, Council Chamber and Ante room. All public meetings are held here, especially if connected with Town Trust Property etc., while the large upper room is available for any Entertainment local or otherwise on application to the caretaker.

The Church Mill is another useful building, this was formerly a disused and ruined cloth mill, and purchased by the Revd Henry Sewell, Vicar, for a few hundreds, was converted into a three storied hive of usefulness; from whence the hum of many happy voices outpours—the first floor consists of the Boys' Church Sunday School with raised platform and grand piano; second floor, Church Institute, where on payment of a small sum quarterly, members are admitted, supplied with Newspapers etc., besides having the use of bagatelle and billiard tables, smoking is allowed but no betting, coffee or cocoa may be obtained. The upper Story or "Top Room" is used for Girls' Church Sunday School and is also furnished with a grand piano; here meetings are held—sewing classes—social teas—and many amusements.

Sir Isaac Pitman formerly lived in Wotton-under-Edge, and had a house in Orchard Street: he is known as the inventor of Phonography and has laid under tribute, not only newspaper men, but every reader of a speech as reported by his system of Shorthand, which has contributed so much to the general accuracy of the reporting of the present day. He may be regarded as one of the Benefactors of Mankind. Knighted in May, 1894. The arms of Wotton are the "Woolpack" still seen in Church Street over the entrance to Hugh Perry's Alms Houses, above the following words—

```
           DEO · GRATIA · FVNDA—
  
   WHICH · FOVNDER · WAS · HVGH ·
G  PERRII · ESQVIRE · AND · ALDERMAN · OF · THE   T
L  CITTY · OF · LONDON · WHO · WAS · BORNE ·      O
O  IN · THIS · TOWNE · AND · BESIDES · THIS ·     R
R  GVIFT · GAVE · MANY · GOOD · GVIFTS ·          I
I  ✢ FOR · THE · GOOD · OF · THIS · TOWNE ✢       ·
A        ANNO · DOMINY · 1638
                  | H. P. |
```

Wotton-under-Edge is famous for its longevity. In August, 1864, Elizabeth Hill of the Alms House passed away, she was known as Nurse Hill and was 104 years of age, her husband reached the age of 100, with the exception of sight she retained all her faculties—a year before her death she could read and sew, Mrs Gardiner of Long Street, Wotton, at her 100th year 10th April, 1892, retained all her faculties and was a bright specimen of holy waiting, she died aged 101.

---o---

THE MANOR AND OTHER ESTATES.

This Manor was a member of the great lordship of Berkeley, at the time of the general survey, but there are no particulars of it recorded in "Doomsday Book" than that there are " In Untune fifteen hides and half a yard land." Roger de Berkeley possessed it in the reign of William the Conqueror, and it descended with the Manor of Berkeley, till the death of Thomas, fourth Lord Berkeley. This Thomas married " Margaret," daughter of " Gerard Warren, Lord Lisle," by his wife " Alice" daughter and heir of Henry, Lord Tyes, with whom he had a very great estate. Thomas, Lord Berkeley and Margaret his wife were buried in Wottton-under-Edge Church, 1416, leaving an only daughter, Elizabeth, who married Richard Beauchamp, Earl of Warwick; she was heiress to the whole estate of the Berkeley family, but James, Lord Berkeley, son of James, younger brother to Thomas, Lord Berkeley, was *heir male*, and as the Berkeley estate descended by heir male only, James was the rightful heir; but Elizabeth's husband, Earl of Warwick, being in Berkeley Castle at the death of his wife's father, seized all deeds and writings that concerned the estate, thus making it difficult for James, Lord Berkeley, to prove his title. Richard Beauchamp died leaving three daughters, co-heiresses. " Margaret," the eldest, was wife to John, Earl of Shrewsbury, and their son, " John," was afterwards created "Viscount Lisle." He, with his descendants, prosecuted their pretensions against the Lords of Berkeley, and Thomas Talbot, Viscount Lisle, son of John, lost his life at Nibley Green in a fatal battle. Thomas Talbot, Viscount Lisle, resided in the Borough of Wotton-under-Edge in "Manor or Lisle House" by the church. There are still remains of his Lordship's House; the "Cloud" was the carriage entrance, and the gate to the Church still bears the name of "Keep Gate" or the "Portico." Very recently, the dungeons and subterranean passages in Lisle House were blocked up; one of these

Lisle House Entrance.

passages leading under the "Cloud" was discovered in an outlying cottage, behind the fireplace, the occupants using it as a receptacle for wood, coal, etc., the cottage being pulled down about 1883. It is traditionary that these passages were sufficiently lofty to enable knights in full armour, mounted on their prancing steeds, to shelter from enemies in their dark recesses, and disappearing

"It seemed as if their mother earth
Had swallowed up her warlike birth."

A tower on the remaining **rampart** wall surrounding the courtyard is *now* a shady summer **bower**, in an old-fashioned sweet-scented flower garden.

The following are extracts from some curious letters which passed **between the** last Viscount Lisle and Lord William Berkeley, respecting the settlement of the 192 years' law suit. Viscount Lisle sent a challenge to William, sixth Lord Berkeley, **wherein he desired him** to fix a time and place for deciding the **suit by the sword.** Lord Lisle's challenge commences thus—

"William, called Lord Berkeley,

"I merveille ye come not forth with all your Carts of Gunnes, Bowes with other Ordinance, that ye set forward to come to my Manor of Wotton to bete it down upon my Head—I let you witt, ye shall not nede to come so nye, **for** I trust to God to mete you **nere** home with English men of my own nation, ..."

To **this challenge Lord Berkeley** returned **answer:—**

"Thomas **Talbot,** otherwise called Viscount Lisle, **not** long continued **in** that name, **but** a new found thing, brought out of strange Countrys, . . . where Thou requirest me of knighthood that I should appoint a Day, and mete thee in the mydway betwene My Manor of Wotton and My Castle of Berkeley, there to try betwixt God and our two Hands all our Quarrels, and **Title** of right . . . For thou art in a false Quarrel and **I in a** true Defence **and Title.** . . Fail not to-morrow to be at Nibley Greene **at eight or** nyne of the Clock, and I will not fail to mete thee."

The parties met on March 20th, 1470, with about 1,000 men. A furious engagement ensued, 150 men being slain. Lord Lisle was fatally shot in the mouth with an arrow (while lifting his vizor), by "Black Will," a forester from Dean Forest, the rude miners having poured from there to assist Lord Berkeley. The victorious Lord Berkeley then hastened to Wotton, rifled Lisle House, and carried away deeds, furniture, and **valuables** to Berkeley Castle. In Edward III's reign Lord Berkeley laid out £100 (**which was** then considered a great sum) in repairing **his** house in **Wotton.** During the contentions of the Berkeleys and the Lisles James, Lord Berkeley came from his castle, brake gates and doors of the Manor House: sawed, hewed and cut in two the timber of the roof and galleries; razed the walls and vaults, tore the iron from the windows, carried away hinges, gutters, leaden pipes, and occasioned an expense of 4,000 marks in repairs. At last, Lady Ann Berkeley in preparing for the ten days visit of King Henry VII to Berkeley Castle, pulled down the hall at Wotton House to assist in making the roof of the great kitchen at the Castle; and this seat which had been "*a Queen of Houses*" to the family for 280 years, wholly perished, and when John Staunton purchased the fee-farm of the site from Henry Lord Berkeley, gilded bricks, stones and pieces of timber were dug up in the reign of James I, (Smythe's MSS.) "Court Orchard" garden allotments were part of the Manor grounds, the word "court" signifying such. The House was restored on the old foundations in the Jacobean style of architecture, and is now, in a good state of preservation, and to those who love the quaintness and memories of olden times besides a comfortable home is a very interesting place.

———0———

HISTORY OF THE ADVOWSON OF THE PARISH CHURCH OF S. MARY THE VIRGIN, WOTTON-UNDER-EDGE.

The Vicarage and Rectory of the mother Church of Wotton-under-Edge together with her two chapels of Symondsall and Nibley belonged originally to the Abbess and Nuns of Berkeley until the time of Edward the Confessor, (A.D. 1042 to 1066) and thence it passed to Earl Godwin and his son King Harold until the Conquest 1066 from which time it passed to the Crown and to Roger de Berkeley of Dursley and his descendants, who held the same in fee-farm rent with the great Manor of Berkeley under the two Williams, Henry I and part of the reign of Stephen; at which time it was given with that Manor to Robert Fitzhardinge and his heirs, upon whose founding the Monastery of S. Augustine, Bristol, it came to the

WOTTON-UNDER-EDGE.

Distant view of Church.

Church Pinnacle

Abbot and Convent thereof by his gift, together with all the other churches of the Manor

There is a grant of Appropriation (circa A.D. 1172) from the Bishop of Worcester, in whose diocese it then was, to the Abbot and Convent, subject to his rights, and the honest sustentation of the Vicars serving in the said churches in Wotton-under-Edge and Nibley, and so it seems to have continued till the 35th Edward I A.D. 1307; when Edmund then Abbot of that Monastery granted the Advowson of this Church of Wotton-under-Edge with all the rights and appurtenances thereof to Thomas, Lord Berkeley, and Maurice his son and heir and their heirs: and so it descended through the family of Berkeley to William, Marquis of Berkeley who in the 7th year of Henry VII 1492 dying without issue left it to the King together with the Manor of Wotton. On the 17th March, 1504, 19th year of Henry VII. Maurice Lord Berkeley, brother and heir to the Marquis recovered the Advowson from the Crown, on a petition of right. It was conveyed by him to the Monastery of Tewkesbury who appropriated it and endowed the Vicarage by a composition; in the 31st year of Henry VIII 1540, this Monastery was dissolved and seven years later the King gave the Advowson by Letters Patent dated Dec. 11th, 1547, to the Dean and Chapter of the Cathedral Church of Christ in Oxford by the name of "all that Rectory and Church of Wotton-under-Edge with all the rights and appurtenances thereof." (Berkeley MSS.)

The Church is dedicated to S. Mary the Virgin and stands in the tything of Sinwell, it is a handsome and spacious edifice with a lofty battlemented pinnacled tower; it has a nave, north and south aisles, chancel, tower, south porch, and chapel on the north side.

The present Church was erected in the 13th century, remains

of this early building being the arcades of the nave, the doorway of the south aisle, the east window, the window sills of nearly all the church and the tower: the roofs of the church then were high pitched and there were no clerestory windows.

The church was no doubt, a complete and perfect edifice, to which was added, in the 14th century the two lower stages of the present tower (ball flower ornament) and this was again added to, by two more stages in the 16th century. A great change took place after the erection of the present, but why affected no one now can say: possibly the desire to obtain more light caused the erection of a clerestory over the nave arcades, and the insertion of larger windows in the church itself may have induced the men of the 15th century to remove the high pitched early English roofs and windows, and to build windows in the Perpendicular style, to erect clerestories, to place flat roofs covered with lead over the whole building, as they were prior to the third, and much to be lamented era in the History of the Church, which took place in the early part of the 19th century. The roofs and fittings were undoubtedly of oak. Screens existed at the chancel arch, and across the north and south aisles, and altars at the east end of the north and south aisles as well as of the chancel, and painted glass in most of the windows. At the commencement of the 19th century the old oak roofs, the clerestory, screens and the old oaken seats of the nave and aisles were removed; and new roofs and windows, such as are there now were erected: giving a debased character to the Architecture of the Church. In 1838 the chancel arch was removed from its old position to where it now is. In 1882 and 1883 the chancel was restored to its original dimensions by the addition of the present screen, the nave was refloored and reseated, the galleries at the west end were removed, throwing open to view the fine tower arch, and western wall of the nave—in 1890 the remaining portion was refloored and reseated, and now Wotton-under-Edge possesses a Church almost Cathedral in appearance, open always for prayer and praise, and that GOD may bless the efforts of those who have laboured to gain such, giving rich and poor equal right therein, is the prayer of many a worshipper.

Paintings of S. Christopher and other Saints, formerly adorned the western wall. There were formerly several chantries, the Chapel on the north side was dedicated to S. Katherine, tiles with her wheel were found between the floor—one dedicated to S. Nicholas—one to All Saints, and one to the Blessed Virgin Mary. (Revd H. Sewell in Parish Magazine)

The Parish registers date from the year 1571 A.D. and are in a good state of preservation. The present font was subscribed for by several bachelors of the parish, who each paid a guinea towards its erection, it was formerly placed in S. Katherine's Chapel, but now occupies its present place in the western or Tower entrance, being removed thence by subscriptions collected by the Sunday School children of the Parish.

The large handsome tomb of grey marble with two figures engraven on brass plates, is in memory of Thomas, fourth Lord Berkeley, and Lady Margaret, his wife, sole heiress of Gerard Warren, Lord Lisle—he died 1417—she died 1392. The Brass of Thomas Lord Berkeley represents the knight in the usual armour of the period with belt and long pendant; the sword unfortunately is gone: the head originally rested upon its heaume. The most remarkable peculiarity is a collar of mermaids, probably a family badge. In the effigy of Lady Margaret the hair is worn over the forehead only and confined with a gold and silver net-work called a crestine or crespine, a small kerchief is pinned at the top of the head and falls behind: the ornamental work seen round the head of the figure must not be confounded with the head-dress, the head resting on a piece of cloth adorned with sprays, and stretched diagonally over an embroidered cushion having a tassel at each corner, at her feet is a lap-dog with a collar of bells. This Thomas Lord Berkeley was contracted to Margaret daughter of Lord Lisle in 41st year of Edward III and by reason of her tender age—she was only then about seven years old—it was arranged that she should remain with her father for four more years: but sickness happening in the family, they were married in the November following, he was devotedly attached to her, and was so affected by her death, that he went on a pilgrimage and never married again though he was only 38 at the time of her death, The brasses are supposed to have been executed at the time of her decease, and only the date added to his—he was known as "Thomas the Magnificent"—the fingers of both effigies were formerly richly jewelled, there is no inscription on the Altar tomb. (B. and G. Archæological Society)

Round the verge of a grey marble flat stone, which had the figure of a man upon a brass plate fixed upon it now torn off (supposed to be the founder's tomb) are these lines in Lombardic Characters, 1329.

" *Natus in hâc villa cognomine dictus ab illâ,*
Qui Rector fuit hic, aptum nomenq ; sibi sic
R. de Wottoná jacit hic, cui cælica dona,
Impretret ipsa pia pulcherrima virgo Maria. Amen."

Translation.

Here lies R. de Wotton who was Rector here, born In this town from which he took his name—a name Well suited to such an one—Do thou most loving and most Gracious Virgin Mary obtain for him heavenly gifts. Amen.

In the centre of the stone.

" *Es mihi virgo pia, Dux et Lux, Sancta Maria.*"

Translation.

Holy Mary loving Virgin be my Guide and Light.

This Brass represented Richard de Wotton Rector kneeling at the foot of a cross. It exhibited the peculiarity of having a scroll issuing from the hands of the figure, with an inscription of which every letter was separately inlaid with brass; this is one of the oldest brasses in the county, but alas! the brass is gone and only the impression remains.

———o———

THE TASWELL MONUMENT.

This is a mural one, with a high pyramidal back of coloured marble, in front of which, and surmounting the tablet is a small exquisitely sculptured statue in white marble, representing the God "Hymen" in a pensive attitude leaning on an urn, and holding an inverted torch. On the base the sculptor's name

South Doorway.

etc. are recorded. The legend connected with this figure, is, that when on its way from Rome to the place of its destination, the ship which conveyed it, was taken by a privateer, and that thus, finding its way to England, and coming into the possession of the family of the deceased at an opportune moment, it was utilised by being placed on the monument in question. Hence the incongruity of a statue of Hymen forming part of a monument erected to the memory of a deceased clergyman. The Revd William Taswell was many years Vicar of this parish, and was buried August 8th, 1775. This monument was formerly at the East end of the Church but has now been placed over the South Porch door interior.

These lines follow a Latin Inscription to the memory of Thomas Grail who died June 5th, 1669, aged 61.

"Here underneath Interr'd doth lie
One that bids Thee prepare to die
I lov'd in upright Paths to go—
Physick my Practice was, but loe,
Death is too strong for any man,
For Physick and Physitian."

(B. and G. Archæological Society)

Over the South Porch is a Priest's Chamber, the door of Entrance being from the Church at the right-hand side, the door at the left hand, is where a chapel formerly stood, only the doorway remaining.

THE ORGAN.

After the Great Rebellion two eminent organ builders came to this country at the request of the Government, one named Father Smith, with two nephews from Germany, the other Thomas Harrison with his son from France. *Christopher Schneider, a clever German workman in Father Smith's establishment, upon the death of his master, succeeded to the business, and was appointed organ builder to King George 1. One of the first organs of importance, built by Schneider, was presented by His Majesty George 1 to the church of S. Martin's-in-the-Fields, London, in 1726; the sum paid for it being one thousand five hundred guineas. His Majesty at that time was chosen churchwarden for the parish of S. Martin, etc., etc., but becoming tired of the office, in three months time, resigning his post, presented to the church as a farewell gift, this noble old organ, which now stands in the parish church of S. Mary the Virgin, Wotton-under-Edge, having been bought by the Rev. Dr Tattersall, vicar, for the small sum of £200 in the year 1800. It is difficult to understand how the Parish of S. Martin's-in-the-Fields came to part with this magnificent old instrument, and that it was considered a very fine one, there is ample evidence, for Handel was engaged to open it, and was so delighted with it, that he attended the church regularly, and often played the voluntaries himself; it is also surprising that the parish of S. Martin's should part with their royal gift, especially as it still bears upon a panel the following inscription, "THE GIFT OF HIS MOST SACRED MAJESTY KING GEORGE, 1726." After building this organ, Schneider completed one for Westminster Abbey, in 1730, at the price of one thousand pounds; therefore the Wotton-

* Mr Watts.

under-Edge organ was more costly, **its** price originally being **one** thousand five hundred guineas, and these two are the only existing instruments by the celebrated Schneider. The following is the opinion of the great American organist, Mr E. Thayer, regarding Schneider's Westminster organ, "The finest church **organ—in the** full sense **of the** word—that the world contains **is the one in** Westminster Abbey, built by Schneider; by **the finest I** mean the most devotional in its quality **and** effect. I have not heard its like, nor do I expect **to on this** side of the Heavenly Gates." As the Wotton-**under-Edge organ** had fallen into a very dilapidated state, in 1883 it was removed from the oaken gallery built against the tower of Wotton Church, where it had been since 1800, and was thoroughly renovated and enlarged by the well-known firm of Messrs Jones, Fulham-road, London. Additions have **also** been made to it, and it **now** is an organ **of** great beauty **of tone** and considerable power the total number of pipes being 1622. It stands in the south-east end of **the** church, to continue its glorious work of swelling out **an** accompaniment to the glory and praise of GOD.

———o———

MEMORIAL WINDOWS.

The three windows in the chancel **in memory** of three distinct families form **one** complete idea, viz., **the** glorification and adoration of the **Son** of Man. The **north** window to the memory of Mrs Fisher, represents **the** "Annunciation" and the "Incarnation" or birth of the Son of Man; the south window **erected in memory of** Major **and** Mrs Ramsay by their daughters, represents **the** adoration **of** the "Magi," and the east window in memory **of the family of** "Cooper," represents **our** Blessed Lord seated **in** glory receiving the adoration of all sorts and conditions **of** men, and of **angels**; in the upper parts **of** the window are angels offering **incense** before the golden throne; below them, kneeling, are the twelve apostles, doctors, patriarchs, prophets, martyrs, virgins and kings. Thus these three windows bring before our constant notice the worship we should always offer to the "Lamb of God, that takest away the sins of the world."* The three-mullioned window over the chancel was placed there in memory of Anthony Adey, Esq., by his widow, beautifying the eastern portion of the sacred building. The window in Tower is to the memory of Colonel John Blagdon Hale and Jane his wife of Bradley Court, erected by their daughter Jane, and other relations. The subject represents the Ascension of our Blessed Lord.

The rich brass chandelier was presented by William Moore, Esq., to the church in 1763, and on his removal from the parish to Abingdon, he also made a similar offering to Abingdon Church. The house of William and Madame Moore still exists in Wotton; it contains an oaken balustraded staircase, panelled rooms, with oil painted panel over the high mantel shelf. The tower of Wotton Church carries a peal of eight bells, which were re-cast by "Rudhall" of Gloucester; they chime every three hours the favourite tune by Handel "Hanover,"

"Ye servants of God your Master proclaim,
And publish abroad His wonderful Name."

*Rev. H. Sewell in Parish Magazine.

The eight bells are for the time being, supposed to be in the scale of "A," and "old Hanover" sounds very well on them, with the exception of one note, for the theoretical explanation we are indebted to Mr Partridge, the late organist.

Compare the tune with the notes of the scale, and it will be seen that the four lower bells are useless; therefore in order to employ these bells, the tune must begin on the first note of the scale instead of the fifth, this "makeshift" throws the tune out of its proper scale of A. The following gives the tune as at present chimed, except the note *G natural which is not in the scale of A.

*Compare the notes with the scale of A, and it will be seen that there is no G natural on the bells, G sharp being used instead.

There is a certain value in regard to inscriptions on Church Bells, they serve as facts belonging to past ages, sometimes the bells carried nothing but the founder's name and date, ours of Wotton-under-Edge bear the following mottoes.

1 When you us ring, we will sweetly sing.
2 Peace and good neighbourhood.
3 Prosperity to the Church of England.
4 Prosperity to our Benefactors.
5 We were all cast at Gloucester by Abel Rudhall, 1756.
6 Revd Mr William Taswell, Vicar.

7 Through Agustin and Phill Dancy, Churchwardens.
8 I to the Church the living call, and to the grave I summon all.

The family of Rudhall must have been of that class of Englishmen who were called good Church and State people, nearly all their bells bear such epigraphs as the following, " Prosperity to the Church of England," or " May the Church of England ever flourish," also the motto which all will fully endorse, and use their best endeavours to promote,

" Peace and good neighbourhood."

In an old account " Booke " dated 1666, is this entry " Keeping the Clock, ringing the Bell, mendynge the Clock, newcasting the Church Bell, and carrying him to and from Bristol, for mendynge ye Clapper of ye Bell, for lead, forty waights, and a new line for ye Clock and divers other disbursements, £6 5s."

A Mrs Page who lived in Church Street about the reign of Queen Anne, ascended the Church Tower, and leaning over the parapet, lost her balance and fell over, she was however fortunately caught by her quilted petticoat upon the lion-headed gargoyle a few feet below the summit, and there hung in mid air. A rope with a noose was procured, this was lowered and the poor victim, had presence of mind sufficient to place the rope round her, and was drawn up into the tower; she immediately fainted, the reaction was too much for the overstrained nerves.

Sundials on Church Porches are not ecclesiastical features, but their terse mottoes of warning and incentive, and their general air of tranquil serenity put out of the question any doubt as to their propriety, adding a genial though mute invitation to enter: the one on the South porch is not old, neither has it any motto, but simply as reminder of the passing of Time may be regarded with interest.

The Churchyard is a sacred and holy spot, where affection may go forth and cherish sweet memories, and whence contemplation may on the wings of faith, look upward to a brighter world beyond the tomb.

———o———

BENEFACTIONS OF WOTTON-UNDER-EDGE.

Katharine, daughter of Sir John Clivedon of Charfield, and widow of Sir Peter le Veel, married Thomas, 2nd Lord Berkeley, who died leaving her again a widow, she founded a school in 1385, which bears the name of Katharine, Lady Berkeley's Grammar School, in the reign of Richard the Second, and endowed it with 40 marks a year, houses and land. In 1885 a new scheme for the administration of the above mentioned foundation school was drawn out by the Charity Commissioners. The school is now a day and boarding school for boys, the Head Master a graduate of some University in the United Kingdom. No boy is admitted under the age of 8 years, and may remain in special cases until 19. A yearly sum of not less than £60, nor more than £100 is given in maintaining Foundation Scholarships, to six or ten boys, each of the yearly value of £6. Also an exhibition of the yearly value of £50 is given by the Governors, tenable on such conditions as they think fit, at any place of advanced education, approved by them. The following subjects are taught in the school, with English in all its branches, Latin, Mathematics, at least one modern Foreign European Language, Natural Science, Drawing, Drill, and Vocal Music; Greek at an additional fee of not less than £3 a year for each boy, and the principles of the Christian Faith. This School is reported by the Charity Commissioners to be the oldest endowed school in the kingdom. There is also an endowed "Blue Coat School," so called from the costume. Thirty boys received yearly from the Charity the picturesque blue coat, with brass buttons, the leathern breeches, the blue woollen cap with yellow band and "boss," the admiration and delight of the small boys, but the detestation of the bigger ones, when jeered at by the fashionables of the nineteenth century; but this is a thing of the past. The Charity now clothing the same number of boys in warm and comfortable suits. Hugh Perry, Esquire, Alderman of London, a native of this place, built the **Alms** Houses and Chapel in Church Street, in 1638. The Bearpacker Alms Houses are for five infirm old men and five infirm old women; in fact Wotton abounds in charities. There are Alms Houses for

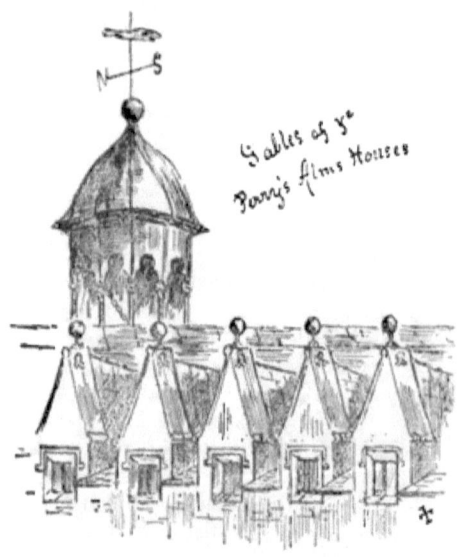

Gables of ye Parry's Alms Houses

Blue Coat Boy.

forty-eight persons or families, and also other charities amounting to about twelve hundred pounds yearly, not including the Warwick Hospital Charity, which was founded by Robert Dudley, Earl of Leicester, (a descendant of the Berkeley family), for twelve poor men wounded in battle, two of which should be from Wotton; and Lady Anne Countess of Warwick, built an Alms House at Cheney, in Buckinghamshire, in Elizabeth's reign, and appointed that two of the alms folk should be from this parish, with a weekly allowance; she also gave the "new Tolsey" to the use of the town. A clock and quaint bell turret is still upon the "Tolsey" building; in "1707 the sum of £2 10s. 6d. was paid

WOTTON-UNDER-EDGE.

Yᵉ TOLSEY DRAGON.

for copper and for making the Dragon and guilding Him," also " Pd Mr Coxe for a jorny from Woster about the clock and diall over the Gate House, 1686." In 1630, Hugh Perry joined with his father-in-law, Sir Richard Venn, in erecting an aqueduct to convey water from a spring in Edbrooke field to the Market Cross. " Thomas Dawes of Bradley, Esqre, gave a fire engine to the town." A new fire engine was given as a memento of Queen Victoria's Jubilee by the Feoffees of the Market Lands 1887.

The Population of Wotton in 1804 was 3,276, the Parish contains 10,998 acres and is about 500 feet above sea level.

The celebrated Rowland Hill, son of Sir Rowland Hill, visited Wotton-under-Edge in 1771, and preached in the Market Place to great crowds of people. He was so charmed with the vicinity that he erected a house, to which he brought his bride, and a chapel called "The Tabernacle," in one of the most romantic situations that can be conceived, and very suitable to a mind exceedingly alive to the picturesque beauties of nature; and Wotton, became his favourite summer residence. The famous Robert Hall once paid him a visit at Wotton, and said of it, "Sir, this is the most paradisaical spot I was ever in," strong as was the expression he did not say too much. (From Sydney's Life of Rowland Hill). Mr Hill was born at Hawkestone in Shropshire in 1744, but as a young man he became associated with the county of Gloucestershire, and was ordained a curate by the Bishop of the Diocese. Like Wesley, however he found the mere discharge of his clerical functions too restricted a sphere for him, and took to itinerant preaching; he drew large congregations, and in some parts of the country laid foundations of permanent work on lines adopted by him. He was a strong supporter of vaccination, on its introduction by Dr Jenner, and himself vaccinated all who came to him. From the pulpit on Sunday evenings, after the sermon, he would say " I am ready to vaccinate to-morrow morning as many children as you choose ; and if you wish them to escape that horrid disease the small pox, you will bring them." There are several Alms Houses connected with Rowland Hill's Tabernacle and a Sunday School ; lately the Alms Houses have been rebuilt on fresh ground in Elizabethan style ; the pointed gables, balconies and woodwork making a pleasant architectural feature in Old Town. It is an old custom in Wotton on May Day to wander over the hills at five in the morning, climbing the rocky paths, over the grassy knolls, through the hanging woods, in search of the budding branches of beech, with which the lovely glens abound, and no house is thought fortunate which is minus a spray of the brownsheathed, silvery green ; washing the face in May Day dew is likewise observed, and many a laugh is raised at the expense of those young people who love their rest more than the merry ramble o'er hill and dale. Some of the May Day ceremonies are as old as the Druids, many older, for they can be traced to heathen festivals held in honour of " Flora." Chaucer tells us that in his time folks rose at one on May morning and sallied forth with music and horn blowing, to welcome the return of Spring. They broke branches from the trees, adorned therewith their balconies and door-posts, and decked their persons with garlands. Even Henry VIII was not above the practice, we are told that he rode forth, accompanied by Queen Katharine, from Greenwich Palace on May Day, to " disport him " at Shooter's Hill. Samuel Pepys informs us that his wife had gone to Woolwich, " to gather May dew to wash her face withal." Every custom should be valued which tends to infuse poetical feeling into the Briton, and to sweeten and soften the rudeness of rustic manners, without destroying their simplicity.

The hills and woods abound in swarms of insects, a perfect garden for the entomologist, who may fling his net over gorgeous butterflies, as bright as eastern skies, while his hours may pass entranced with the melody of the many feathered songsters, the blackbird, the linnet, the lark, the gentle trilling robin, the whole family of finches, the swallow, and last but not least in the musical world, the sweet cadenza of the nightingale, while in the darkening shade the glow-worm's little lamp shines starlike in the dewy grass.

"A nightingale that all day long,
Had cheer'd the village with his song,
Began to feel, as well he might,
The keen demands of appetite,
When looking eagerly around,
He spied far off upon the ground,
A something shining in the dark,
And knew the glow-worm by his spark."

Delightful it is to roam in the woods, to wander from glade to glade, and from thicket to thicket, to reach the innermost recesses, where twisted trees of every imaginable form " make network of the dark blue light of day," so closely are they woven overhead; while all traces of the pathway are lost amid rich carpeting of variegated hues, and trails of ripening ducal strawberries, wild and unrestrained. The hazel tree with its pale, green catkins hung among the primroses and sweet scented violets forms the brushwood, while the delicate " Anemone " or " Zephyr Flowers " enamels the ground, the latter crimsoning with the rude blasts of the cold spring winds. Preeminent in the wood is the " Lily of the Valley "; its lowly home the " Lily bed " is in the shady glen, where to be seen it must be sought, bending its graceful petals in its glossy leaves ; " Solomon's Seal " and the white flowers of the reeking " Garlic " are often mistaken at first sight for this sweet scented flower. Round many a gnarled old root clings the pink streaked " Woodbine," with its trumpet shaped flowers, and " Woodruff " *(Asperula Oderata)* like a waxen frill edges the skirts of the wood. The " Woodderowffe," as spelt by the old authors is commemorated in the rhyme—

" Double U double O double D E
R O double U double F E."

The flower itself is scentless, but no sooner does it dry, than it exhales a pleasant fragrance, resembling new mown hay, yet partaking of the odour of bitter almonds " sweetest when crushed," and crushed the poor flowers often are, for they blossom in such dense profusion that to step, one sacrifices the nodding hyacinth with its dark blue bells and clumps of primroses, whose pale, fresh flowers like stars begem the mossy way. So much for spring and summer ; autumn brings the deep red leaf and the sunset gold of the bramble and a wealth of mulberry-sized blackberries, and many excursions are made " a-blackberrying " and " a-nutting," Nuts may be gathered in handfuls and the whisking squirrel makes a fine larder in the hollow trunk of some old oak ; while many a country oven is heated with a faggot of hazel twigs ; and the streets of the Wotton town are crunching with empty nut shells which the school boys scatter, munching the kernels furiously meanwhile. The meadows are bestrewn with the Snowdrop (Fair Maid of February), the " Lenten Lily " (Daffodil), and the wine-producing " Cowslip," the " Leopard's Bane " (Doronicum), a very rare plant found in the moat field by " Bradley Court " from May to July ; while by the water-courses and mill streams the blue " Forget-me-nots " and golden " Kingcup " vie with the stately " Iris " and slender Bulrush. Moor fowl dart in and out of the sedgy reeds growing by Combe and Hack Mills ; the latter takes it name from " Acker " meaning a ripple on the surface of the water. A beautifully clear, rippling well of water, caught in a stone tank near the Grist Mill,

has medicinal properties, especially noted for strengthening the eyes. "Eglantine," "Clematis," or "Traveller's Joy," with its dark-green leaves and greenish white flowers clings to the hedgerows, suffocating them with its feathery crown; its predecessor, the wild rose, in all its varieties, from delicate cream to deepest rose colour, leaves its scarlet berries to heighten the effect, by a touch of warmer colouring; while from sandy crevices, in the light of the summer sun, flourish the vase shaped "Bindweed," the yellow "Geum," the yellower "Crowsfoot," the "Ragged Robin," the various coloured "Vetch," the fairy "Foxglove," the clear-toned "Campanula," the mournful "Periwinkle," and, with its purple bloom, the "Scabious." The shady lanes are luxuriant with ferns, and rare specimens are to be found. Flowers and ferns gathered by nimble fingers, bound together into bunches, each bunch bearing a text card, or words of cheer and comfort, can be sent to the sick in the Town Hospitals every month from Wotton; the variety of ferns, leaves, berries and flowers, is so great that a hamper full may soon be procured; and Miss Florence Nightingale assures us that nothing so cheers and enlivens the mind of the patient as "flowers, bright flowers," Flowers given in the spirit of Christian love and self-denial, are messengers from GOD; they carry with them the kindness of Him who has sent them to His creatures, and are fitting types of the glorious resurrection.

> "Flowers,
> Minister delight to man,
> And beautify the earth." . . .
> "That man wher'er he walks may see in every step the stamp of GOD."

Petrifactions of marine substances, as the oyster and cockle shells, ammonites (*mollusca*), are discovered easily in this neighbourhood: "it has been a matter of doubt how so many shell fish, and other productions of the deep should be intermixed with the soil of our highest hills, it is now generally believed to have been the effect of the universal deluge." To archæologists the large "coney gore" or Roman settlement will prove an attraction, and also on Coombe Hill the "Ring o' Bells" triplet druidical circles, a remnant evidently of our ancestor's worship.*

* Ring of Baal (?) or Molech, an altar for human sacrifice.

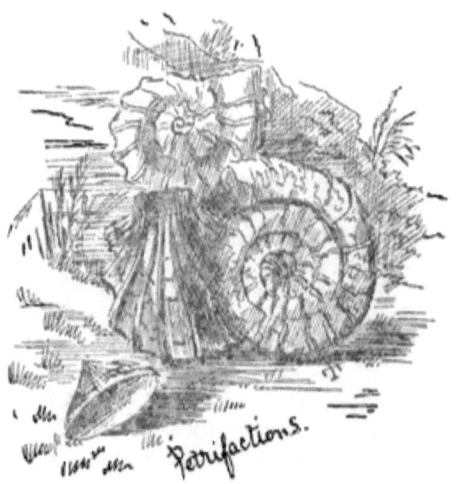
Petrifactions.

The Society of Arts offered a premium for the discovery of the mistletoe on the oak, and had a very fine specimen sent them from an oak in Gloucestershire. The "Brackenbury Ditches" in the West Ridge woods are Roman trenches.

---o---

TITHINGS AND HAMLETS.

"Bradley" gave name to an eminent family to whom it belonged. Hugh de Bradley lived in the reign of Richard the First. This manor was held by Sir Maurice de Berkeley, in the reign of Henry the Fourth, and many of the lands were given by Thomas Lord Berkeley to the Abbey of S. Augustine's Bristol, for which reason the chief messuage is called Canon's Court; and after the dissolution of religious foundations they were granted to the Dean and Chapter of Bristol. "Bradley House" or "Court" is a fine old mansion and celebrated as the house, where Edward II. was confined previous to his removal to Berkeley Castle and it is usually stated, that at the time the king was murdered (Sept. 21, 1327), Lord Berkeley was lying dangerously sick and unconscious at Bradley, one of his manors, and that Sir Thomas Gournay, and John Maltravers committed the horrid deed. Fortunately for Berkeley and for the Barony, this plea was admitted, without much investigation by a jury of twelve Knights, and he was acquitted of complicity in the crime, although the accounts of the steward of the household mention that Lord Berkeley did not arrive at Bradley until Michaelmas, seven days after the murder; to this John Smyth in his " Lives of the Berkeley's" gives credence. There is a fine old avenue of elm trees leading to Bradley Court, and a quaint stone " Dove Cot" as large as a barn, with pointed gable and doorway; inside the stones are built with regular interstices, so making 950 or 1000 nests for the cooing tribe.

Simondshall is the highest ground in this part of the country, eighteen counties may be seen from some parts of it; in Doomsday Book it is recorded "that half a hide in Symondshall belonged to the Lordship of Berchelai!" There are here the remains of an ancient mansion house the residence formerly of the " Veel" family, who came into England with William the Conqueror. Hugh le Veel was in great esteem with King John.

" Combe" lies eastward of Wotton Church, and was given by the Empress Maud to Nigel de Kingscote (ancestor of the Kingscotes of Kingscote), for his services to her in the wars, but that family (as Rudder observes), " was probably dispossessed of it on the change of affairs."

" Sinwell" is comprised of a few straggling cottages by the Warren woods; the latter deriving their name from " Gerard Warren, Viscount Lisle," the house called "The Warren" is a comparatively modern structure, pleasantly situated, and though sheltered with trees, yet possessing a picturesque and panoramic view.

" The Rudge" or " Ridge" is an estate sometimes in ancient writings dignified with the title of manor. It belonged formerly to the Abbey of Kingswood.

Wortley is a distinct tithing where was formerly a Chapel of ease, founded by Thomas Lord Berkeley, dedicated to S.

John in 1356, after the battle of Poictiers, with his prisoners' ransom money, for priests to say "masses for his ancestors, himself and successors." This Chapel has been converted into a dwelling house, the family of the present occupants having resided there over a century. The road to this dwelling house is still named "Chapel Hill" and one buttress remains as a relic of the past.

---o---

NEIGHBOURING PARISHES.

One of the many pretty walks, is through the fields to the interesting village of Kingswood, where are the remains of an old Abbey, and where the "curfew bell" tolls out the hour of eight p.m. Kingswood is a manufacturing parish on the banks of the Little Avon river, Merriford stream, the water of which long ago bore grain in boats to the Abbey, and supplied the monks with trout and grayling. The following History of Kingswood Abbey is culled from some old writings, and is nearly verbatim:—

"In the year of our Lord 1131, the 31st of King Henry I, Walter de Clare founded an Abbey of Cistercian Monks at Tintern in Monmouthshire, and dedicated it to the Virgin Mary. This convent being desirous to enlarge their order, applied themselves to William de Berkeley, with a petition to found an Abbey of the same order at Kingswood, then in the County of Wilts, of which he was the proprietor; William yielded to their request (it being thought meritorious in those days to erect religious houses), and founded and endowed a Monastery at Kingswood, to the honour of the Virgin Mary, in 1139, which was partly supplied with monks from Tintern, and his concession or grant was confirmed by a charter from Maud, the Empress, daughter to King Henry I.

"Wars breaking out between King Stephen and Maud, gave the monks great uneasiness, and they chose to remove from Kingswood to some quieter situation, in order whereto they purchased a ville called Hazeldean, now a hamlet of Rodmarton, in Gloucestershire, of John of S. John's, to whom

King Stephen during the wars had made a grant of it, though the lands belonged rightly to Reginald of S. Walerie, who had taken part with Maud. But when the wars were over, everything was to be restored to the rightful owners; Reginald then ejected the monks, and repossessed himself of Hazeldean. The monks thus dispersed made perpetual complaints to Reginald of the injury done them, and by their teasing and importunity at length so prevailed with him, that he promised he would restore Hazeldean, and bestow on them some other lands, if they would but transfer Kingswood Abbey thither, for, he told them, that through a penance enjoined him by the Pope, he was obliged to found an Abbey of the Cistercian order. To this proposal the monks so far consented, that they chose to divide their society, and one moiety of the religious order was to stay at Kingswood, and the Abbot with the rest to settle at Hazeldean, and so they kept both places in their possession. They had not been long fixed at Hazeldean, when they found themselves incommoded for want of water, of which there was a great scarcity, so upon Reginald's motion they removed again to a place called Tetbury, where he generously bestowed some lands upon them, near which was a perennial spring that would never fail to supply them with water. This removal of the monks from Kingswood gave some umbrage to Roger de Berkeley, heir to the above mentioned William, and he thereupon drew up a remonstrance to the King on this affair, complaining of this injury to his father's foundation, and setting forth that Kingswood was left to him by his predecessor, as a noted Abbey, but was now only held as a grange to Tetbury; the main body of monks being removed thither, he insisted that he might either have his land again, or the monks be recalled and settle at Kingswood. The King thought this reasonable, and yielded to his request, but by the interposition of the General Chapter of the Cistercians, who petitioned against the remonstrance of Roger, the King was prevailed with to resolvent the order, and it was determined that Kingswood should be made a grange to Tetbury, but that mass should be constantly read at Kingswood by some one monk, with Roger before mentioned, to give him twenty-seven marks and a half in silver, and one mark to his son, and thereupon Roger, by his Charter, ratified the contract, and confirmed to them his father's gift. Affairs being in this posture there was a convocation held at Kirchstead, where many Abbots met, among the rest Philip, Abbot of Elemosyne; Henry, Abbot of Waverley, and Pagan, Abbot of Tetbury. Here, after the debates about which they met were ended, the Abbot of Waverley proposed to restore the Abbey of Kingswood and replace the monks in it, and to take upon himself the direction of the monastery; to this the Abbot of Tetbury, being a weak man, gave his consent, but without the knowledge of his convent, or the assent of the Abbot of Tintern, who, when they heard of it entirely disallowed and opposed, and a great deal of litigious disputes followed upon it, but in the conclusion it was decreed in a meeting of the Cistercian Abbots at Kingswood, that the Abbot of Waverley should recall the four monks whom he had sent to Kingswood, and remove all his goods and chattels, and Kingswood should return again to its former use as Tetbury Grange; yet there was still left in the monastery several monks, converts, clerks, and laicks, with Roger the founder, who was present at these accommodations. At length, the monks at Tetbury not so well liking their situation, having scarcely room enough for the commodious settling of an Abbey there, and finding great inconvenience through the scarcity of wood for firing in those parts, being forced to fetch their fuel from Kingswood which lay at a considerable distance, chose to remove back to Kingswood, but the building there being not sufficient for the reception of their number, Bernard of S. Walerick, founder of Tetbury Church, requested and obtained from Roger de Berkeley, lord of Kingswood, forty acres of land at Merriford, a place bordering on Kingswood, near the waterside, and there they erected a new Abbey, about A.D. 1170, and transferred the convent of Tetbury. The ruinous remains of this Abbey are still standing near the brook, and the old Abbey which stood about a mile to the south, was partly pulled down to furnish materials to build the new, yet a small chapel belonging to it is still partly remaining, called to this day 'the old Abbey.'* From this time Merriford took

* About the year 1830 the ruins of the old Abbey were pulled down, and a cottage built on the site.

the name of Kingswood, and here the monks having erected a handsome church and chapel, dedicated to the Virgin Mary, remained till the dissolution of their Abbey, which was in the 31st year of King Henry VIII reign. The church of Kingswood was demolished with the Abbey, and the materials sold, but the Lady chapel was left standing for the use of the parishioners. This account was taken partly from the annals of Waverley in the Catonian Library, and partly from the 'Monasticon Anglicanum,' vol. 1, folio 811, and which exhibits the charters, and has preserved an old record belonging to the Abbey, which was said in 1651 to be in the hands of Mr John Smith of North Nibley."

Adjoining the site of the Abbey, can be seen the fishpond, the banks of which are still perfect, beyond facing south the sloping field still known as the Abbey Vineyard. The meadow called the Vineyard in Wotton-under-Edge, belonged to Kingswood Abbey. Robert Lord Berkeley (1189 to 1220) gave a water mill and divers lands adjoining at Wortley, and land called Bradpen and pasturage for one hundred sheep, rents etc. at Wortley, also his "pretious gold ringe and many other things."

The last Abbot of Kingswood was named William Bowdeley, and at the time of the dissolution there were 13 monks there. Thomas Lord Berkeley, who died 1243, was an especial benefactor to the Abbey in the reign of Henry III. Over the kitchen chimney piece of the Abbey were carved a Tiger, a Hart, an Ostrich, a Mermaid, an Ass and a Swan; the initials forming his name *Thomas*. Elizabeth only daughter and heiress of Thomas Lord Berkeley (whose fine altar tomb is in Wotton-under-Edge Church), and wife of Richard Beauchamp Earl of Warwick was buried in Kingswood Abbey 1422, to whose memory a goodly tomb of marble was erected by her husband, according to her will.

"The Cistercian order of monks was founded by Robert of Neoles, at Cisteaux, in Burgundy, in 1098, and introduced first into this country at Waverley in Surrey in 1128. By their rule all their churches were dedicated to the Virgin Mary, and they so arranged the position of their houses that there should not be another house of their own order within a certain distance; their dress was a white habit with a narrow scapulary with a gown over, except while travelling, when they had a black gown; they have also been called 'White Friars,' or Bernardines from S. Bernard, who so much raised the fame of their order. They were ordered to abstain from all decoration or ornament in their church or service, no peal of bells was allowed, or stained glass in their churches, they were not allowed a crucifix in their services, only a plain painted wooden cross. They were especially enjoined to live in the country, avoiding the crowd of towns; living thus, they employed themselves in practical as well as devotional duties, to the cultivation of the land, which belonged to them, the preservation and repairs of the buildings on their estates, the work of their church, and the education of the people. This necessitated the employment of a number of lay brethren; these were admitted under a special vow. The sanitary authorities of those days were very strict, and necessitated that the arrangements of the conventual buildings should depend on the waterflow; the houses being built over running water, or a feather stream from the nearest running water conducted a flow under, or adjacent to, the kitchen and domestic offices." (J. R., Member of the British Archæological Association.)

"The Cistercian Abbot, Stephen Harding, in 1114 forbade chasubles in his church to be made of anything but fustian and plain linen; the monks wore boots, the canon shoes and the friar sandals. Land, in Slymbridge, belonged to the Abbey of Kingswood, the Rector of Slymbridge pays £10 yearly to Magdalen College, Oxford, for choir music, and annually on the first of May the choristers ascend the tower of that princely building at five in the morning to sing a eucharistic hymn which "floats down in a sweet calm like the music of the spheres."*

The place of Kingswood gave name to a forest of large extent; the office of keeper was formerly annexed to the constableship of Bristol Castle, Humphrey Stafford was constable 1 Edward IV, and Humphrey Cook keeper of the forest 1660; but the whole is now "disafforested and vested in different

---

* Holman Hunt has immortalized this in his beautiful painting executed in 1891.

proprietors." Previous to the year 1830 there was a very old Lane or Bridle road named the Trench Lane leading from Abbey to Abbey, it commenced at a place called Squall's Lake (now dry) winding through the Trench Fields to the old Abbey: its sturdy old oaks and densely thick and tangled underwood, a harbour for owls and bats, made it a solitary, gloomy, almost solemn old road—the cottagers living near bore the name of "*Trench Owls.*"

"Dinnywick" (or burial place) is the name of a rather large field on the left hand side of road leading to Hillesley from Kingswood, it has a mound in it and is interesting, whether containing remains of those slain in battle, or as a Danish Barrow. The Church of Kingswood, dedicated to the Holy Trinity and erected in 1723, is a stone building Early English, with tower and clock containing a set of tubelar bells, which may be heard at some distance; the latter is quite a modern possession; the bell which rings "Curfew" is dated 1706, its motto is "God save our Queen and Church." The churchyard is quaint, and in front of the Church Porch are some pollard wych Elms now ten in number formerly twelve, representing the Holy Apostles. The Candelabra is the gift of Richard Blinco, distiller of Bristol 1723.

———o———

NEWARK PARK,

Near Wotton-under-Edge in Ozleworth Parish formerly belonged to the Monastery of Kingswood, and Newark House is built with the stones from Kingswood Abbey and partly from stones pulled from crosses in the neighbourhood by Sir Nicholas Pointz in the reign of Edward VI. It is situated on an eminence commanding extensive views; a subterranean passage exists, supposed to lead from thence to Kingswood Abbey. Here Snowdrops grow in great profusion, a favourite flower in a Monastic garden sacred to the Virgin Mary; and many a shady dell especially in the West of England, where not a stone of the old convent remains, the Snowdrop still blossoms in the Spring telling us of a vanished garden. There would probably be a small Monastic building or Ark of refuge here, as the name "New Ark" suggests. There is a legend, that some monks from Kingswood sought safety in the subterranean passage leading to the "New Ark" where they perished, and on the eve of every Saint's Day their Spirits appear in solemn procession with lighted tapers and clad in Cistercian vestments, gliding from a panelled wall in the present Newark House, they slowly pass through the room, across a passage and down the beautiful staircase chanting softly as they go. There is a little fort at Newark called the "Broome," famous for the duel between Sir William Throkmorton and Walter Walsh then of Little Sodbury.

———o———

TYNDALE'S MONUMENT.

On the Midland line from Gloucester to Bristol may be seen distinctly the monument on Nibley Knoll erected to the memory of William Tyndale, translator of the Bible; the little village of North Nibley, two miles from Wotton, claims to be the birthplace of this Christian Martyr, who perished at Vilvorde, in 1536. There is no record of his early studies, and it is no great stretch of imagination to suppose that he received the rudiments of languages at the Wotton-under-Edge Grammar School, before entering as a student Magdalen College, Oxford. He afterwards became chaplain to Sir John Walsh, lord of the manor of Little Sodbury; and almost within sight of the spot where he had spent the years of his childhood; in the old-fashioned dining hall of the manor house of Little Sodbury, he first conceived the idea of his great work, the translating of Holy Scripture into his native tongue; a *fac simile* of his translation is preserved in a glass case in the upper story of the monument on the Knoll, which visitors are permitted to see by paying a trifle to the custodian, who lives in the village. "It having been found that the copy of the New Testament which was placed in the Chamber of the Tyndale Monument

Tyndale's Monument.

was becoming seriously damaged, in consequence of the decay of the case in which it was deposited, the Revd J. Hardyman of Old Town Chapel, Wotton-under-Edge, in 1890 had a substantial oak case made in which the Book, which is black lettered and dated 1595, and is of great value, is now placed. He also had another case made in which he has deposited a *fac simile* copy of the letter written by Tyndale while in the prison at Vilvorde, in Flanders, shortly before his martyrdom; the contents of both cases which have glass fronts so that the contents may be seen, are of great interest, and are in the chamber at the top of the tower. The copy of the New Testament was a gift of the Revd G. S. Spencer, formerly Minister of the Old Town Chapel, and was placed in the Tower at its opening." (Local paper) The church of Nibley or Nybley, anciently written "Nubbelei" and "Nubbeleigh" signifying "cloud water" or obscure place, is an old stone building in the early English style, with a low embattled tower at the west end, with six bells, and a small spire over the chancel and the nave for a sanctus bell. Mr John Smythe, of Nibley, wrote

many valuable historical manuscripts, which he was forty years compiling; they have never been printed, and are in possession of the Berkeley family, however a few copies were printed in 1887. He lived at Warren's Court for more than forty years and died 1641 and was buried at Nibley. A flat stone in the floor near the pulpit much worn still shews the Latin inscription commemorating his name. In 1607 Smythe commenced building a new house at Small-combe Court (pulled down in 1790) over the entrance he placed a stone with date and engraved letters   N. M.   M. H.   which are the initials of the
S. P.   N. C.

Latin couplet.   *Nunc mei mox hujus*
Sed postea nescio cujus.

Translation.

T'is mine to-day; to-morrow (perhaps) my heirs';
But after whose? Let him reply who dares!

It proved prophetic, the Nibley estates passed entirely out of his family; this stone may still be seen over an arched doorway, which was erected on the site of the house in 1807. During the building of the house in 1607 the family fool of Berkeley Castle satirized Smythe's growing wealth and importance by tying the Castle to the Church, to prevent as he said the Steward from carrying the Castle to Nibley to build his new house with.   (James H. Cooke)

———o———

BERKELEY.

BOLING—"How far is it my lord, to Berkeley now?" (Seven miles from Wotton—)
PERCY—"There stands the castle, by yon tuft of trees," will as fairly now describe the situation of the fortress, as when the immortal Shakespere penned the lines. The best view of the Castle is from the park, it was built in 1134 on the remains of an ancient nunnery which existed in the time of William the Conqueror, and was the last castle which held out

VIEW OF THE SEVERN FROM THE NIBLEY ROAD

against Oliver Cromwell. It consists of a keep and an inner court yard, surrounded by buildings of castellated form; it has a noble hall and chapel. In this Castle the unfortunate Edward II was murdered; above the steps leading to the keep is a room called the dungeon, containing the original furniture, and is shewn as being the place where the foul deed was committed, and gives the Castle tragic celebrity. The church built in the early English style is separated from its tower by a vacant space of 146 feet.

Berkeley will be for ever renowned as the birth-place of Dr Edward Jenner, the introducer of vaccination; he is buried here, and a statue erected to his memory in Gloucester Cathedral; a handsome stained glass memorial window is placed in the chancel of Berkeley Church also. The horns of the original cow from which he took the lymph are preserved in Gloucester Museum. Through the kindness of Lord and Lady Fitzhardinge, who reside in the Castle, visitors are allowed to see the interesting fortress, and can obtain orders for viewing it certain days in the week.

Three miles from Berkeley are the docks at Sharpness and the "Severn Sea," with the white sails of a merchantman or pilot boat upon its broad waters. Sharpness is the entrance to the port of Gloucester, large steamships discharge grain in these docks; there are also some well kept pleasure gardens, where one may inhale the gentle southwest breezes, and wander through the leafy paths, which the late Dowager Countess of Berkeley claimed as her pleasance, belonging now to the Canal Company. A strong iron bridge crosses the river at this point, uniting the two banks, over which spin the trains slowly *en route* for Chepstow and Tintern. On the road from Berkeley to Wotton is "Stancombe," where are the remains of a Roman villa, and specimens of tesselated pavement were removed from thence for preservation to the Museum, Gloucester. A farewell glimpse of the "Silvery Severn" is obtained from "Bournestream," "The Bordering Stream" or "Streamstream," where stands a sundialed gabled house on the Nibley highway, which in the reign of James I was occupied by a "yeoman," the house standing in the midst of its own grounds. Bournestream House possesses a mottoed sundial, the words "I mark none but sunny hours." Horatia K. F. Gatty to the Editor of The Standard in reference to the motto at Sackville College, "*Horas non numero nisi serenas*," as occurring at no less than fifteen places in the same form, and the same thought, variously clothed in English words. "Perhaps," she remarks, "the happiest version is at Bournestream House, Wotton-under-Edge, 'I mark none but sunny hours.'"

———o———

INTERESTING PROCEEDINGS AT BERKELEY CASTLE.

The Corporations of Berkeley and Wotton-under-Edge, which have existed from time immemorial, ceased on the 25th March, 1886, in pursuance of the Municipal Corporation Act, 1883. In consequence of this it was suggested by each Corporation that the maces used by their respective bodies should be handed over to Lord Fitzhardinge, who is Lord of the Manor of Berkeley and Wotton boroughs, to be kept by him and his successors as heirlooms. On this being made known to his lordship, he invited both Corporations to lunch with him at Berkeley Castle, at the same time suggesting that he could then receive the maces of both Corporations. The following are copies of the addresses which were handed over with the maces to Lord Fitzhardinge:—

"To the Right Hon. Francis William Fitzhardinge, Lord of the Manor of Berkeley Borough in the County of Gloucester."

"The Corporation of the Prescriptive Borough of Berkeley in the County of Gloucester, now dissolved by the Municipal Corporation Act, 1883, respectfully request your lordship to receive back the mace presented to them by your ancestor, the Right Hon. George, Earl of Berkeley, in the year of our Lord, 1661, to hold the same to yourself, your heirs and successors, Lords of the Manor of Berkeley Borough, as an heirloom. As witness our hand, the 25th day of March, 1886." (Here followed the signatures of the Mayor, Aldermen and Sergeant-at-Mace of Berkeley).

WOTTON-UNDER-EDGE. 51

"To the Right Hon. Lord Fitzhardinge, Lord of the Manor, etc.

"We the undersigned, being the late Mayor and Aldermen of the Borough of Wotton-under-Edge, in the County of Gloucestershire, who as a Corporation, were dissolved by the operation of the Municipal Corporation Act, 1883, on the 25th March last, beg to express to your lordship the deep sense of regret we feel at the severance of the tie which has existed between your lordship's noble house and the Borough of Wotton-under-Edge for upwards of 600 years, and at the same time we take the opportunity of handing to your lordship the silver mace which was presented by your lordship's noble ancestor, Augustus, Earl of Berkeley, for the use of the Corporation in 1747, to the intent that it may be for ever preserved as an heirloom by yourself and successors, Lords of the Manor of Wotton Borough, and as a memorial of the interest and patronage your noble house formerly took and exercised in the Corporation of Wotton-under-Edge. Signed at Wotton-under-Edge, this 10th day of May, 1886." (Here followed the signatures of the Mayor, Aldermen, and Sergeant-at-Mace of Wotton Borough).

On the procession arriving at the Castle they were shown into the fine old baronial hall, where they were received by Lord Fitzhardinge. The last Mayor of Wotton, Mr J. F. Blake, and Mr D. Legge, senior Alderman of Berkeley, in the absence of Mr T. P. Bailey, the last Mayor, read the above addresses, handed over the Maces, and added some suitable remarks, expressing regret at the termination of the connection between his lordship as Lord of the Leets of Berkeley and Wotton and those ancient boroughs, and presented the maces to him.

Lord Fitzhardinge thanked them for so doing, and said he reciprocated their feelings of regret at the severance of the connection alluded to. His lordship then produced the old mace of Berkeley, which was returned to the Lord of Berkeley in 1661, when the present mace was given, which was dated 1300. The Chalice or Godwin cup, which is dated 1066, and is the oldest known piece of plate in England, was then filled with champagne, and the noble chairman proposed the healths of the last Mayors of Berkeley and Wotton, and having drunk to the toast from the cup, sent it round the company.*

Lord Fitzhardinge is willing to retain the mace at Berkeley Castle, agreeing that it shall be shown to visitors on days on which visitors view the Castle, and that if ever it is closed to the public, he will deal with the mace as the Charity Commissioners shall direct.

* From a Bristol Paper.

ALDERLEY,

A small parish, two miles south from Wotton, situated on a rising ground, was formerly the utmost bounds of the forest of Kingswood; in Doomsday Book the name is written "Alrelie." Two small brooks bound the parish on the north and south, unite, and run from thence to Berkeley to "join the brimming river" Severn. Alderley is remarkable as being the birthplace of that great lawyer, Sir Matthew Hale, Lord Chief Justice of the King's Bench. He lived in the time of the greatest civil commotion this country ever knew, yet he carried himself so uprightly as to be equally admired and esteemed by all ranks and conditions of men. He was a most pious gentleman, and was never absent from divine service on Sundays during thirty six years. Mrs Bunyan, wife of the famous John Bunyan, travelled on foot to London, hoping to be the means of obtaining her husband's release from prison, and tried in the simplicity of her heart to get access by petition to the House of Lords, and was informed that the only parties who could effect her object, were the Judges of the Assizes. One of these proved to be the celebrated Sir Matthew Hale, whose beautiful Christian character soared larklike up from the odiousness of his position; he heard her patiently, and expressed great sympathy for her sufferings and domestic conditions, but explained to her, that her husband could be extricated only, by application to the King. While Twisden, the other Judge, treated her angrily and asked " will your husband leave off preaching? if he will do so, then send for him." " My Lord" replied she, " he dares not leave preaching as long as he can speake." Alderley Church was rebuilt in 1800, the old clock now standing in the tower was the gift of Sir Matthew Hale, dated 1673; a monument of black and white marble covers the grave of this just man, who died on Christmas Day 1676, and was buried at Alderley. The Church is dedicated to S. Kenelm, the tower is very old, dating from 1458, the Bell is dedicated to the Virgin Mary. A Monument in the Churchyard is to the memory of Thomas Stanton, Minister, exiled in the reign of Queen Mary and returned again as Minister in 2nd year of Queen Elizabeth's reign. Miss Marianne North the accomplished Traveller, Botanist and Artist, died at Mount House, Alderley. A few years ago she presented to the Nation an exhaustive Botanic Picture Gallery at Kew Gardens, most of the pictures were painted by herself from Nature, the pictorial record of her expedition round the world. At Alderley her flower garden was beyond description a luxuriant mass of loveliness. Leland says "A Man, native of Alderley, in 1225, feigned himself to be 'The Christ;' and according to the sanguinary jurisprudence of that age was brought to Oxford and *Crucified*: instead of treating him as a poor maniac." An artist will find in Alderley and Wortley, much that constitutes the poetic beauty of landscape painting, and in the neighbourhood of "Tor Hill" are some lovely little pieces of scenic effect.

Adjoining Alderley is the pretty little village of Hillesley, where a Flower Show is held yearly, having the reputation of being one of the longest standing in the country. The present Church is a modern building consecrated in 1851, it is built upon the site of a former Chapel of the same dedication (Saint Giles), which had been converted into four tenements for the poor, (according to Sir Robert Atkins' history of Gloucestershire, dated 1712). Many curious remains were found in digging the foundations of the present Church, such as massive mullions of windows, and also the old font which was broken; this Chapel of Ease was one of seven daughters belonging to the Mother Church of S. Mary, Hawkesbury, with Tresham and Little Badminton, the two latter are the original Chapels. The Church of Saint Mary, Hawkesbury, is an ancient stone building of various dates, built principally in the perpendicular style, has a nave, south aisle, chancel, and handsome embattled tower. All that is known of its early history is that about the year 680 a College was founded for secular canons by Oswald, nephew of King Ethelred, that in 984 King Edgar at the intercession of the Bishop of Worcester introduced Benedictine Monks, and that its impropriation belonged to the Abbey of Pershore in Worcestershire, from the time of William the Conqueror to its dissolution. The building as it now stands dates from the Saxon period, and contains work of every period from that time to the present. The only Saxon remains are the bases of the shafts of the inner doorway of the north porch, it was re-opened 9th April, 1885, after its restoration. Hawkesbury was formerly called Stoke Hamlet or Stock (Saxon) the stem, or main body, being the Mother Church, the seven daughters or Chapels of Ease were Hillesley, Tresham, Kilcot, Upton, Saddlewood, Ingleston and Little Badminton. An old church notice at Hawkesbury without date, on the notice board of the northwest porch of parish church, "It is desired that all persons that come to this Church would be careful to leave their Dogs at home, and that the women would not walk in with their Pattens on."

At Hawkesbury Upton, four miles from Wotton-under-Edge, on the brow of a hill, commanding a magnificent view of the surrounding country, is a fine monumental tower, erected to the memory of **General** Lord R. E. H. Somerset, 1846, **built** upon the first **land** the Somerset family possessed in England, all their property having **been** previously in Wales; this point may have been originally chosen for a beacon, as the "Wyndcliff" in Monmouthshire, is visible on **a** clear day. The Lower Woods lie in the valley below, also **the** "Sodbury Vale." At Little Sodbury is a very strong camp, of an oblong **form**, about 320 yards in length. Some think this camp, **to be** Danish, others Roman, but certain it **is that the** army of Edward IV occupied it a short time before **the** battle of Tewkesbury. Foxes swarm in these great coverts, which are of large extent, and belong, with a small exception, to the Duke of Beaufort, K.G. The Lower Woods extend about three miles in length and one in breadth, are strong in under covert, at times very difficult to pass through, owing to the length **of the** grass. 'Tis a fine sight on a winter's morning to see the **huntsmen** and hounds meet preparatory for the chase, looking **as fresh as the morn.** Edward the Confessor, though more of a monk than **a** monarch, took great delight in following a pack of swift hounds, so saith William of Malmesbury

Four miles from Hawkesbury Upton is Badminton Park, with patriarchal oaks and elms spreading their embracing arms around, whilst hundreds of red and fallow deer rest beneath their shade, or startled with some mimic **sound, rush** like the wind into distant space. Badminton House, the seat of the Duke of Beaufort, is a fine old mansion with a private Chapel attached, dedicated to S. Michael, built in classic style, consecrated in 1783, consists of chancel, nave of four bays, aisles and a western tower containing three bells, **it** has **a** highly enriched ceiling, **a font** of beautifully veined marble, the floor of chancel is Florentine mosaic, the altar steps **of jasper** and verde antique. There are some handsome **monuments** here, white marble studies, life size by Rysbrach, also **the tomb** of Lord Raglan who was buried **in** 1855. Badminton House has a fine collection of paintings brought by the **early** Dukes, examples of Raphael, Guido, Carlo Dolci, Salvator **Rosa**, (including the satirical piece which cost him his expulsion from Rome), Tintoretto, Caracci, Da Vinci Teniers, Holbeins and Jansen, Sir Joshua Reynolds, etc., etc.; also a collection of

Badminton Park.

fourteen family portraits in succession from John of Gaunt onwards, which were removed hither from the earlier seat of Raglan Castle. There are two noted oaks in the park called the "Fitzherbert" and the "Duchess." What Lord Macaulay's "History of England" asserts of Badminton in 1685 will prove equally true now, two hundred years later, "The fame of the kitchen, the cellar, the kennels, and the stables was spread over all England."

OZLEWORTH,

Formerly written "Wozelworth," is about two miles east from Wotton, the road to it being up "Lisle Hill" and past the "Black Quarrs" or "Quarries," where some of the caves vie with Cheddar in glistening stalactites. Ozleworth is situated on the verge of a hill, with woods adjoining, and is remarkable for the number of foxes killed in one year during Queen Elizabeth's reign, which amounted to 231. The church is an ancient Saxon edifice, divided into two compartments by a beautiful Saxon arch with chevron mouldings, and an octagonal tower rising from the centre, containing one bell. "Newark Park" near here, was restored in the reign of Edward VI with the stones which composed Kingswood Abbey.

----o----

BOXWELL,

Three miles from Wotton, has a fine boxwood, about forty acres in extent, probably the largest in the Kingdom. In it is a well dedicated to the Virgin Mary; a tradition exists of a nunnery here before the Conquest. The old Manor House was the court house of the Abbots of Gloucester, under whom the Huntleys were lessees, and purchased the freehold of Sir Walter Raleigh, to whom it was granted by Queen Bess; during the Civil War it was frequently the resting place of Prince

Badpath Church

Rupert. The church is an old stone building in the Early English style with campanile tower, there is also a very curious Early English font. Leighterton is a hamlet and chapelry of Boxwell, here is a barrow opened by Matthew Huntley, Esquire about the year 1700, with three vaults, in each of which was found an earthen urn, containing burnt human bones; there is also a smaller one at Boxwell, whereon is a large upright stone above six feet high.

Newington Bagpath Church dedicated to S. Bartholomew, has a peculiar square, campanile tower; it is an old stone building, very quaint; the living is attached to "Oldpen" or "Owlpen." The "Owlpen" property is one of the oldest in the county; an original grant to the Owlpens by Earls Berkeley. The Daunts, a family of eminence in England and Ireland, acquired the property by marriage with the heiress of Owlpen.

---o---

KINGSCOTE,

Is about six miles from Wotton-under-Edge. The inhabitants have a tradition that there was once a city here of the name of Kingchester. As tradition has generally some truth for its formation, it serves at least to show that this village has been anciently distinguished by camps or some eminent buildings. Remains of tesselated pavement, Roman coins, etc., have been ploughed up at different times, and a large stone statue of "Minerva," and other antiquities. Colonel Kingscote is Lord of the Manor and chief owner. A short distance from Kingscote is Calcot Barn which was built by the Abbot of Kingswood in the reign of Edward I. Within the doors was a bas-relief called "Balaam and his Ass;" Bigland's M.S.S. referred to it as being 130 feet long, and capable of holding 900 loads of corn, there are indications of its having once been used for sacred purposes.

---o---

ULEY,

About four miles from Wotton north-east. Uley, Celtic,

"Uhella," "highest,"—in Doomsday Book recorded as "Eunelage," which means "watery place," is taken no doubt from the numerous springs which rise here. Part of the hill on the north side of the village shoots out in a rocky head, and is united by a narrow neck of land to the open plain adjoining Nympsfield. This is a Roman camp "Uley Bury," the highest in the South Cotswolds, is very strong by situation, commanding the all but impregnable slope below. A great military road has been cut round the promontory sixty feet in width; coins have been found here of the time of the Emperors Antonius and Constantine. A fine chambered tumulus, or place of sepulchre, has also been discovered at Westhill in this parish. The local name is Hetty Peglar's Tump.

A short distance from Uley is Nympsfield; an eminence here contains an ancient burial place which was explored by the Cotswold Naturalist Club in 1861, and 16 bodies were found. The view from this spot overlooking the Vale of the Severn, the Malvern Hills, and into South Wales is one of the finest in the kingdom. The old turnpike road from Bath to Gloucester leads down Nympsfield hill, which is very steep. Colonel Massey, famous for his memorable defence of Gloucester, against King Charles I, being disgusted at some of the Parliamentary proceedings, deserted their party in 1659, and formed a design of seizing Gloucester, being disappointed and forced to take refuge in a little house near Simondshall. There he was seized by a party of horse, who mounted him before one of the troopers, and carried him towards Gloucester; but in going down Nympsfield Hill, Massey tumbled himself and the trooper from the horse, and being a stout, strong man, and his guards slightly intoxicated, made his escape under favour of a dark, tempestuous night.—(Rudder).

---o---

From FROCESTER HILL,

A few miles beyond Nymphsfield is obtained a splendid view, wild, rugged, and romantic. "Frowcester" old name, a Roman settlement. The village is little and old, once a residence of the Abbots of Gloucester, and possessing a fine barn 184 ft. by 29 ft. with 12 bays, and good trusses. Queen Elizabeth honoured this village with a visit, and stayed a night at the Manor house, as appears from an entry in the parish register as follows: "*Hoc anno 1574 die festo Laurenty martyris Serenissima Regina n'ra Elizabetha hoc n'rm oppidatum accessit et invisit, in eoq; in Ædibus Georgie Huntley armigeri, comiter, benigneq: et fum' a cum humanitate tractantis p'noctarite, indeq, Barkleyum Castellum concessit,*" *i.e.*, On the day of the feast of Saint Lawrence in the year 1574, our Most Serene Queen Elizabeth, came into this our town, and lodged in it that night, at the seat of George Huntley, Esqre., by whom she was elegantly and splendidly entertained, and afterwards she went to Berkeley Castle. There, at the suggestion of the Earl of Leicester, she made havoc by chasing and mercilessly killing the Earl of Berkeley's red deer, thereby offending his lordship.

---o---

DURSLEY.

Six miles north from Wotton, is one of the five ancient boroughs of Gloucestershire. The ruins of a Castle formerly belonging to the Berkeley family are still visible, part of the materials have been used in building the Manor house at Dodington. Leland observes that it had a good moat, or in his own words "a metely good dyche round it and that it was chiefly built of towse stone, full of pores and holes lyke a pumice." There is a handsome market house of free stone in the centre of the town, built in 1738, on which is a statue of Queen Anne. The eldest sons of the Earls of Berkeley took their title of Viscount from this town, the eldest son being called "Viscount Dursley." On the south-east side of the churchyard are many springs, which rise perpendicularly out of the ground like boiling water, they are called the "Broad Well"; but in old writings the name is "Ewelm"—a Saxon word meaning the "head of the spring." The neighbourhood is noted for quarries of "tuffa" or "puff" stone, which when first dug is soft and easily worked by the mason, but on exposure to the weather hardens and becomes very durable. Berkeley Castle is built with part of it.

STINCHCOMBE HILL.

Two miles from Dursley and four from Wotton, commands an extensive view of the surrounding country, which can scarcely be excelled on the whole continent of Europe, so says a writer in the *Saturday Review*. Sham fights and military reviews are held here yearly.

———o———

TORTWORTH PARK.

Four miles west from Wotton-under-Edge, contains the seat of the Right Hon. Earl Ducie, Lord Lieutenant of the county. The most remarkable production of the parish is "The Tortworth Spanish Chestnut," probably the oldest tree now standing in England. It is a grand old monument of the remote past, still hale and full of vigour, may possibly have been planted by the Romans. It measures 19 yards in circumference, and Atkyns mentions it as a famous tree in King John's time, and Mr Evelyn to have been so remarkable for its magnitude in the reign of King Stephen, 1135, as then to have been called the "great chestnut of Tortworth," and as it long fixed the boundary of the manor, it probably took its beginning before the reign of King Egbert, 800. An old tradition gives three periods to the oak and chestnut, viz., three hundred years growing, three hundred years standing, three hundred years decaying. Roman coins and fragments of pottery are frequently found here, and the remains of a camp exist on a hill in the Park called the "bloody acre," and on the south side of the hill are remains of a vineyard.

———o———

CROMHALL,

Four miles from Wotton possesses an old Roman road, and there are remains of a strong encampment or Roman villa on Lord Ducie's land, where probably Roman soldiers were posted to protect the road. This camp lies at a convenient distance from two others on Sodbury and Horton Hills, the road was also well guarded by a regiment of soldiers at Wick,

There is also the site of a hermit's cell, called "Anchor" or "Anchoret Hill," and the site of a mediæval monastery or priory or grange, belonging to St. Austin's, in Bristol. During the four hundred years of Roman rule in England, this country was highly civilized, beautifully straight roads were made, with villas and post houses at a distance of five miles apart, public and other baths were also numerous. It is doubtful if any of our modern roads are as good as those made sixteen hundred years ago; highways are a sign of civilization, a means of human intercourse, a finger post of the times.

———o———

WICKWAR,

Four miles south-west from Wotton. "Wic" or "Wicken" signifying a village or dairy farm, afterwards called "Wickwar" from the family of La Warr, who for many generations were lords of the manor. In this neighbourhood are rocks of very compact and ponderous stone, which from its colour is called "white lays," a species of marble. The Church is said to have been erected by one "Woolsworth,✝ who likewise built a house near the pool; against the east end of this house is the figure of Saint John the Baptist in an erect posture, pointing with his left hand towards the Church, and over him this inscription in ancient characters,

"STE IOHES BAPTISTA ORA . . . . . and under the figure—

IN YE ZERE OF OUR LORD GOD M°CCCC°IIIJ

SCORE AND XVI TRINETE MONDAY XXII DAY OF MAY,"
(viz :- 1496). *see Fosbroke*

———o———

CHARFIELD,

A Railway Station on the Midland Line from Gloucester to Bristol is two and a half miles from Wotton-under-Edge, an omnibus conveys passengers from that town for the various trains. The old Church of Charfield is of great antiquity, and one of the few in this county that possesses a hagioscope or

✝ "an eminent clothier of the place" *Fosbroke*

squint. The registers date back to 1586, are beautifully kept, a few curious entries occur, families still living in this parish can be traced back more than 200 years. There is a large Mound near Charfield, this tumulus is known as Hellbury Hill or Alderman's Bury, probably a Saxon burying place; it was slightly excavated under the direction of R. B. **Hale**, Esqre, but nothing was discovered.

---o---

WOTTON-UNDER-EDGE.

Why should we leave our sea-girt isle?
Where mountains frown, and valleys smile,
Where furious rivers roaring leap
With foaming wrath, out o'er the deep,
Or flow through some wild rugged glen,
But seldom visited by men,
Where one **may roam** from morn to e'en
Amidst the **ever** changing scene,
At every step new beauties rise,
At every turn **a** fresh surprise ;
Why should we leave such scenes **sublime,**
To seek them in a foreign clime?
Why waste time in another land,
Whilst here such beauties are at hand?
Know—that our scenery can compare
With any we can find elsewhere ;
For there are numerous spots to **view**
Yet still unknown but to the few,
And ne'er hath tourist ever trod,
Along the unfrequented road ;
Yes. Such are num'rous, still they **seem**
Uncared for, as a midnight dream.

There's **one,** methinks I see it now
From **off the** low hill's flattened brow,
The town lies smiling at my feet.
The eye can trace each well-known street,
Distinctly see the new Town Hall,
The Chipping flag-staff bare and tall,
The Blue Coat and the Grammar School,
A few old mills for weaving **wool,**
The Tabernacle's slender spire,
Which some old residents admire
More for the sake of Rowland Hill,
Than for artistic taste or skill,
Beyond this, on a shelter'd ledge,
The church of Wotton-under-Edge

Appears in view with massive tower,
From which the bells chime each third hour,
In tones melodious, sweet and clear,
The noble tune of " Hanover."
This fine, old, ancient Gothic pile,
Is rich and elegant in style.
And stands amidst some fine old trees,
Through which now floats th' autumnal breeze,
Causing their foliage to unfold
Rich treasures of unburnished gold;
Within, without, the tombstones lie,
To teach the living they must die;
And oft are curious fossils found
Deep, in this consecrated ground—
Beyond this, in the vale below,
Through which some sparkling waters flow,
Are many neat and smiling cots,
Enshrin'd midst trees on sunny spots,
And graceful clumps of elms are seen,
And golden grain, and pastures green—

I see the other vale below,
Through which the Severn's waters flow,
A river this, expansive, wide,
And o'er its surface vessels glide,
For many a ship, and skiff and boat,
Upon these tidal waters float.
This valley is of vast extent,
Rich, fertile, and luxuriant.
O'erspread with woods, and shady groves,
And lovely glens, and sheltered coves,
With noble mansions, castles, towers,
With sunny dells, and fragrant bowers.
And towns and villages complete
The picture lying at my feet.
Far in the distance to the West
Is many a hill and mountain crest,
Dim, and obscure, of sombre hue,
Co-mingling with ethereal blue,
In southern Wales these mountains rise,
Their outline blending with the skies,
So faint I scarcely can descry,
Which is mountain, which is sky—
All, all is beautiful around
This hallow'd, this enchanted ground.

Go—when the hills and vales below,
Sparkle 'neath the noontide glow
Of Autumn's sun. Go—reach this ridge,
And gaze o'er Wotton-under-Edge.

JOHN D. TAIT.

THE BERKELEY MANUSCRIPTS, AND THEIR AUTHOR—JOHN SMYTH.

By JAMES HERBERT COOKE, F.S.A.

Re-printed, with some additions and corrections, from the Transactions of the Bristol and Gloucestershire Archæological Society, Vol. V., 1880-1.

OF the several existing collections of materials for that much-to-be-desired History of Gloucestershire, which is still said to be "looming in the future," there are, perhaps, none so important as the compilations of John Smyth, which remain in their original manuscript in the Evidence Room at Berkeley Castle. They have for many years been so closely secluded from public view that even their existence is scarcely known, except to readers of Bigland and Fosbroke; while the brief and desultory extracts from them, given by those writers, afford a very inadequate idea of the mine of antiquarian wealth which they contain, and of the extent to which our stores of knowledge of the History, Topography and Genealogy of Gloucestershire might be enriched by it. The present noble lord of Berkeley has, however, very kindly allowed the manuscripts to be shown on two or three occasions, and they have also been examined and reported upon by the Royal Historical Manuscripts Commission; so that I think we may be justified in anticipating that they will one day be given to the world through the press.[1] In the meantime, some account of these works, and of their author, may not, perhaps, be unacceptable to the members of a Society which has been formed expressly to work in those fields in which Smyth was so early and so industrious a labourer.

[1] They are now (1883) being printed by Lord Fitzhardinge's kind permission, for the Bristol and Gloucestershire Archæological Society, under the Editorship of Sir John Maclean, F.S.A.

Fosbroke[1] says that John Smyth was the son of Thomas Smyth, of Hoby, co. Linc.,[2] second son of William Smyth, of Humbstone, (? Humberstone) in the same county. He was born in 1567, and educated at the Free School of Derby, whence he came in 1584, to attend upon Thomas, the son and heir of Henry, 17th Lord Berkeley, then 9 years old, at Callowden, near Coventry, where the Berkeleys at that time chiefly resided. Smyth's position in the family is well illustrated by an anecdote which he himself tells us, and which is worth repeating, because it also gives us a glimpse of the life and manners in great households at that period. Speaking of Katherine lady Berkeley,[3] he says ;—[4]

"For the awing of her family, (I say not regulating the expense according to the revenue,) and the education of youth, shee had no compeere, which I could much inlarge in many perticulers. I will only mention one instance : That as myself in 26th Elizabeth, (then about seventeen,) crossed the upper part of the gallery at the Fryars in Coventry where shee then dwelt, and walked having a covered dish in my hands with her son's breakfast, wherewith I was hastening, and thereby presented her, then at the farther end, with a running legge or curtsey, as loth too longe to stay upon that duty, shee called mee back to her, and to make ere I departed one hundred leggs, (soe to call them,) at the least ; and when I had done well, and missed the like in my next assay, I was then to begin againe ; and such was her great noblenesse to mee therein, (then a boy of noe desert lately come from a country schoole, and but newly entered into her service,) that to shew mee the better how, shee lifted up all her garments to the calf of her legg, that I might the better observe the grace of drawing back the foot and bowing of the knee."

Notwithstanding this menial service there is no reason to doubt that Smyth was of good family, and his position, according to the ideas of those days, not unbecoming gentle birth ; the immediate attendants of persons of high rank were all gentlemen, and are always so styled in household

[1] History of Gloucestershire, Vol. I., p. 468.
[2] I suspect that this a mistake for Leicestershire, "Linc." having been misprinted for Leic. There is no such place as Hoby in Lincolnshire, though there is a Humberstone, but there are both Hoby and Humberstone in Leicestershire. It is also much more likely that Smyth would be sent to the Derby School from the latter place than from the N.E. corner of Lincolnshire, more than 100 miles further off.
[3] She was third daughter of Henry Howard, Earl of Surrey.
[4] Lives of the Berkeleys, Vol. III., 849.

accounts and orders **of the period. The service of** great families was, in fact, much sought **after** for younger sons **and others** who **had their way to make** in the world, both **as a** means of education and training in courtly **and** martial accomplishments, and as an introduction to a career in life. **At the same** time with Smyth, and in the same capacity, came also to Callowden, William Ligon, a scion of the family of Madresfield,[1] who was nearly related **to** the Berkeleys, being the great-grandson of Anne, **only daughter of** Maurice, **the 13th lord.** The two boys seem **to** have been as much the **companions as the** attendants of the **young Berkeley, the three pursuing their studies together under the same tutor, Mr.** Edward Cowper, of Trinity College, Oxford. **About this time Lord** Berkeley, **for purposes of** retrenchment, **removed his family** from Callowden, to the **old** White Fryars' **Monastery, at** Coventry, which **had been converted** into a private residence since the Dissolution, having taken it on **a** lease for three years, **reducing his establishment from** 90 to 70 servants of all **grades. In** Feb., **1589, Thomas Berkeley** and his two companions were entered of Magdalen College, Oxford, where they remained studying together for three years, after which Smyth removed to the Middle **Temple as a student of common** law.

On the **completion of his** studies **at the Temple, Smyth** returned **to the Berkeleys, and** in 1596 became Steward **of the** Household, but exchanged that appointment the following year for the more dignified and lucrative office of Steward of the Hundred and **Liberty of** Berkeley. At the **same time he settled at** North Nibley, four miles from **Berkeley, having** married **a** well dowered widow **there, the relict of John Drewe, Esq.** He also took a **lease of** Warren's Court and **the** lands belonging to it, an estate belonging to the Free School of Wotton-under-edge, which was founded and endowed in 1385, by Katharine, Lady **Berkeley.** The crown **had for** many years laid claim to the **endowments of this school,**

[1] Now represented by Earl Beauchamp.

under the statute for the Dissolution of Chantries, in 1 Edw. VI., whereby much trouble and expense had been occasioned. By the exertions of Smyth, and chiefly at his expense, a decree in chancery was obtained, by which these claims were set at rest, and the school re-incorporated under new regulations suitable to the requirements of the time.

In 1607 Smyth commenced building a new house[1] at Smallcombe Court, in Nibley, an estate which he purchased from William Tracy. Over the front entrance he placed a stone on which, with the date, were engraved these letters:

N.M.   M.H.
S.P.   N.C.

which are the initials of the words forming the following rhyming Latin couplet;

NUNC MEI,   MOX HUJUS,
SED POSTEA   NESCIO CUJUS.

which may be freely translated or paraphrased thus:

> 'TIS MINE TO-DAY; TO-MORROW, (PERHAPS) MY HEIR'S;
> BUT AFTER, WHOSE? LET HIM REPLY WHO DARES!

An appropriate memento of the instability of all earthly possessions which in Smyth's case proved prophetic, as the Nibley estates passed entirely out of his family before the end of the next century. This stone, with its inscription, may still be seen over an arched doorway, which was erected on the site of the house in 1807, by John Jortin, Esq., to whom the estate then belonged. During the building of this house, it is said that the family fool at Berkeley Castle satirized Smyth's growing wealth and importance by tying the castle to the church with string, to prevent, as he said, the steward from carrying the castle to Nibley to build his new house with.

In 1609 Smyth's wife died, and he soon afterwards married Mary, elder daughter of John Browning, of Coaley,

---

[1] A view of this house, which was pulled down about 1790, is given in "Atkyns' Gloucestershire."

of an ancient family long settled there, who had for many
generations held the rectory and great tithes of that parish
under lease from the Abbot of S. Peter's, at Gloucester, and
subsequently from the crown, until they were purchased in
fee by John Browning in 1616. By this lady Smyth had five
sons and four daughters, whose descent he, with some pride,
traces through the Brownings and Fitz-nichols, to Nicholas,
the second son of Robert Fitzharding.[1]

Besides the Stewardship **of the** Berkeley Manors in
Gloucestershire, Smyth was subsequently appointed Steward
of the Borough and Manor of **Tetbury,** of the Manor and
Hundred of Bosham, in **Sussex, of the** Manor of Melton
Mowbray, and some others **in** Leicestershire and elsewhere,
belonging to Lord Berkeley, **the** fees and emoluments of
which must have considerably increased his revenue, and go
far to account for his frequent purchases of land. He gradu-
ally acquired a considerable estate at Nibley, which descended
to his eldest son. He also occasionally bought property else-
where, which **he** sold again, **probably** making **a** handsome
profit, **as the Gossington** Hall manor and estate, **in the parish
of Slimbridge,** and an estate at Newport, **near Berkeley,
besides** others. Smyth has been vilified as having "feathered
his own nest at the expense of his **master,"** an imputation

[1] **I have an old** painting which I believe contains the portraits **of**
Smyth's second wife and her eldest child. It is on panel 26 in. by 21 in.,
and represents a lady in the high-crowned hat and stiff ruff or frill of the
period ; the child wears a crimson dress and an elaborate cap of point lace,
and carries a "coral," **in** its left hand ; it occupies the lower left hand
quarter of the picture and appears to have been painted in subsequently.
In **the upper** right hand corner is the inscription in faint white letters,
"Ætatis suæ 35, 1612," and over the child, "primo anno ætatis sui ; "
the latter inscription exactly corresponds with **the** age of John, the eldest
child of Smyth, who was born, according to the Nibley Register, on the 12th
September, 1611 ; there is no clue to the age or date of birth of Mrs. Smyth,
as the Conley Registers **of** that period are not in existence, but Smyth himself was 45 years old in 1612. I have traced this picture back through its
former possessors to the **sale of the** Smyths' furniture and other effects,
which took place at **the** "Great House" in Nibley, on 28th February, and
three following days, **in** 1792, **of which there is an** advertisement in the
Gloucester Journal, of Monday, Feby. 27 in that year.

for which there is not the smallest foundation, and which his writings afford ample evidence to refute. The Berkeleys indeed were most liberal to him, as he frequently and gratefully acknowledges,[1] but Fosbroke[2] is wrong in his conjecture that part of their bounty was a grant of the land then newly reclaimed from the Severn in the parish of Slimbridge, which was the subject of an unsuccessful suit by the crown against Lord Berkeley, in 1638, defeated mainly by Smyth's exertions; Smyth[3] shews that this land was held on lease from Lord Berkeley, by Oldisworth and Thorpe, from whom he bought a third part or share, for the purpose of contesting the claims of the inhabitants of Frampton-on-Severn to rights of common thereupon, in which he was successful. Smyth's will, however, shews that at the time of his death he held some highly beneficial leases of Micklewood Park and Haw Park, now two farms on the Berkeley estate, as also of Holt's farm and Westridge Woods, both belonging to Lord Berkeley. These were probably granted him in recompense for extraordinary services in which he was often employed, such as the final settlement with Lord Lisle of the famous great Lawsuit, in 1609, the negotiation of the marriage of Theophila, the grand-daughter of Henry Lord Berkeley with Sir Robert Coke, son of the Lord Chief Justice, in 1613, and some troublesome and long-continued chancery suits, touching tithes and rights of common at Callowden and Wiken, in which he was a commissioner for Lord Berkeley. Smyth's services as Steward of the Manors were remunerated by fees paid by the suitors in the courts over which he presided, and not by salary from the lord, and it was probably easier for

[1] He especially mentions (Lives of the Berkeleys, Vol. III., p. 833) the great kindness of Lord and Lady Berkeley, in visiting him during a dangerous sickness, with which he was laid up at Gloucester for six weeks, in 1608, and in providing for him a "Unicorn's horn and a Bezoar stone," two rare and costly remedies not unknown to the older pharmacopœia, besides "exquisite jellies," by which, he says, "my daies seem repryved to this present."

[2] Preface to his "Extracts from Smyth's Lives of the Berkeleys."

[3] M.S. "Description of the Hundred of Berkeley," p. 328.

Lord Berkeley in those days to pay for extra work by grants of land than in money, as well as more acceptable to Smyth. The whole tenor of his life and works displays an earnest, constant, and single-hearted devotion to the interests of the family he served, and a generous appreciation and liberal recognition of it on their part, which are highly honourable to both the parties.

In 1621 Smyth was member for Midhurst, in the parliament which impeached and degraded Lord Chancellor Bacon. Fosbroke says that he became a violent Puritan, but there is not the slightest evidence of this in his writings, and there are many expressions and allusions in his works which exhibit an entirely different feeling.

John Smyth died in 1641, and was buried in Nibley Church.[1] His eldest son, who married Anne, the daughter of Sir Edward Bromfeild, succeeded him in his employments under the Berkeleys, and resided at Smalcombe Court, which his father settled on him at his marriage. George Smyth, his grandson, was the Author of a Translation of Pliny's Panegyric on the Emperor Trajan, which he published in 1702, with a long dedication of the work to H.R.H. the Princess Sophia, of Hanover. He was High Sheriff of Gloucestershire in 1711, and another George Smyth in 1770. The latter built the present mansion at Nibley, called the Great House, in 1763. Nicholas Smyth married the heiress of Owen, of Condover Hall, in Shropshire, and was High Sheriff of that county in 1772. His son, Nicholas Owen Smyth, took the surname of Owen in addition to his own, and sold the Nibley estate to John Jortin, Esq., in 1803. He died unmarried in 1804, when the male line of the Smyths became extinct. The Condover Hall estates went to his sister, Anna-Maria,

---

[1] A flat stone in the floor near the pulpit, much dilapidated and worn, still shews the remains of a Latin inscription, commemorating his name, age, and date of death, to which is added the motto, "Solus Christus mihi sola salus." There is also on the south wall a handsome mural monument, bearing a kneeling figure in the costume of the period, under an arch, with an inscription, in memory of his first wife.

married to Edward Pemberton, Esq., whose son and heir, Edward William Smyth Pemberton, dying without issue in 1863, they were inherited by Reginald Cholmondeley, Esq., who is the grandson of another sister, Caroline Elizabeth. This gentleman has lately submitted his valuable family papers to the examination of the Historical Manuscripts Commission, whose fifth report contains very full notices of them; amongst which are many original letters and other documents of John Smyth and his son, highly interesting and important to the future Gloucestershire historian.

Of Smyth's manuscript works, perhaps the most important is his Lives of the Berkeleys, in three volumes, folio, containing 933 closely written pages. In this work he gives a complete biography of every Lord of Berkeley, from Robert Fitzharding down to his own time, twenty-one in number. The events and transactions of each lord's life are given, with some variations, under the following heads; 1.—His birth and course of youth. 2.—His husbandries and hospitalities. 3.—His foreign employments. 4.—His recreations and delights. 5.—His purchases and sales of land. 6.—His law-suits. 7.—His alms and devotions. 8.—His miscellanies. 9.—His wife. 10.—His issue. 11.—His seals of arms. 12.—His death and place of burial. 13.—The lands of which he died seized. 14.—The application and use of his life. The statements under each of these titles are verified by marginal references to the documents and authorities from which they are taken. The first heading contains particulars of each lord's place and date of birth, and the manner of his education and bringing up to man's estate. The second, third and fourth describe his habits and amusements, and his military and other public services at home and abroad. The fifth and sixth detail his dealings with his estate. The seventh was always a long one with the Berkeleys, who were, in all their generations, remarkable for their benefactions to, and endowments of, the church, and monastic and other charitable institutions. The eighth contains such events and transactions as do not come under any other heading. The ninth and tenth state full particulars of the lady he married, her family and dower, and also of their issue, including the descendants of younger branches, down to the latest period. Besides the pedigrees of the various branches of the Berkeleys, Smyth also gives those of no fewer than 232 other families connected, directly or indirectly, with them. Under the eleventh head are described the seals of arms and other devices used by each lord, with drawings of many of them, cleverly done with the pen. The twelfth, "last scene of all," gives the date and circumstances of his death and place of burial, and is followed by a schedule of the lands of which he died seized, taken in most instances from the Inquisitiones post mortem. Then follow some reflections on the lessons to be drawn from each life, in which our author dispenses his praises or censures most impartially and unsparingly; the "moral" being for the benefit of the young George, Lord Berkeley, who was in his 17th year at the period of the completion of this work, A.D. 1618.

It is scarcely possible to over-estimate the archæological value and importance of such a compilation as this. The Berkeleys were actively concerned in almost all the civil and military transactions in our history; they have been allied by marriage with all the great families of England; and they have, at one time or another, possessed property in almost every English county, except the most northern. Their family annals, therefore, furnish the most valuable illustrations of our national History, Genealogy and Topography. The daily life and occupations of successive generations are also described with a truth and fidelity which seems to bring our forefathers and their doings actually before us, as with a telescope, or "through the looking-glass," and give such an insight into the manners and customs of past times as has seldom or never been afforded us.

If the "Lives of the Berkeleys" has more national and general interest, Smyth's "Description of the Hundred of

Berkeley" is perhaps of still greater importance as regards Gloucestershire. The Hundred of Berkeley was anciently accounted one-fourth in extent, and one-third in value, of the whole county. The book, which is one folio volume of 426 pages, is prefaced by a general descriptive and historical sketch of this part of Gloucestershire. Then follows a very remarkable collection of old Gloucestershire Proverbs, shewing colloquial and other peculiarities, highly interesting to students of philology and folk-lore. The rest of the work contains a complete history and description of every parish and place in the Hundred. The accounts of the manors commence with Domesday Book, and are traced down through successive owners to Smyth's own time. Every freehold also is minutely followed out from its original grant, and the pedigrees of its owners given, down to its possessor in 1640, and for this purpose Smyth seems to have obtained access to the title deeds of almost every family. There are also full accounts of the Churches and Religious Foundations, and other monuments of antiquity, with frequent notices of any natural or other remarkable peculiarity in each parish. This work is most essential to the compilation of a thoroughly comprehensive History of Gloucestershire; but it may be said that if the history of the rest of the county could be carried out with the same amount of research and minuteness of detail, we should have a county history of a character hitherto scarcely even attempted.

Smyth has also left a folio volume of the names of all freeholders owing suit to the Three weeks Court, or Court of Pleas, of the Hundred of Berkeley, and for what lands they owe such service. Also another volume of the Tenures by Knight's service under the Berkeleys; these books would be of great value and utility in tracing Gloucestershire pedigrees. He also wrote a History of the Borough and Manor of Tetbury, and another of the Manor and Hundred of Bosham, in Sussex, which seem to have been lost.

It is scarcely necessary to say that Smyth is not always absolutely correct in his statements, but his mistakes are few and far between, and never affect any important point. Whenever he says anything that seems to conflict with other authorities, I have generally found reasons for believing Smyth to be right and the authorities wrong. His labour, patience and industry in these compilations must have been enormous. In his day a journey to London was a two days' ride on horseback, and none of the facilities for research with which modern antiquaries are favoured were in existence. The ancient records of which he made such good use were not, as now, gathered together into one Public Record Office, with every facility for their search and perusal, but were scattered about in various places, some in the Tower, others in the Rolls Chapel, the Chapter House at Westminster, or the repositories of the various courts. The Calendars of State Papers, the various publications of the Rolls series, and the writings of Nichols, Nicolas, Sims, Marshall, and other active and zealous workers have made a comparatively "royal road" to the study of historical antiquity in our day. By those who experience the value of these helps, the labours of John Smyth may be appreciated, but it is only by the publication of his works that full justice will be done to his memory.

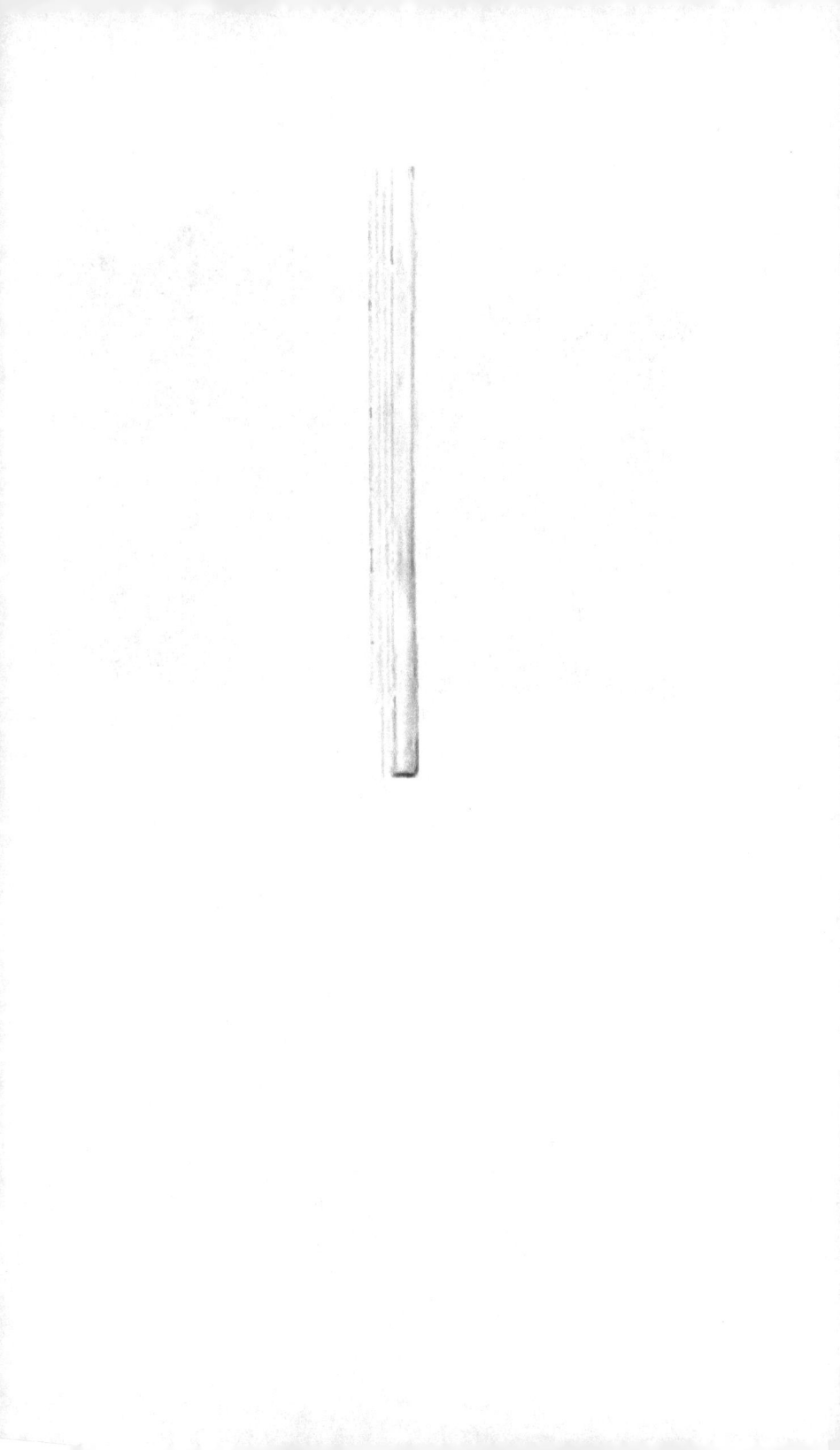

Wotton

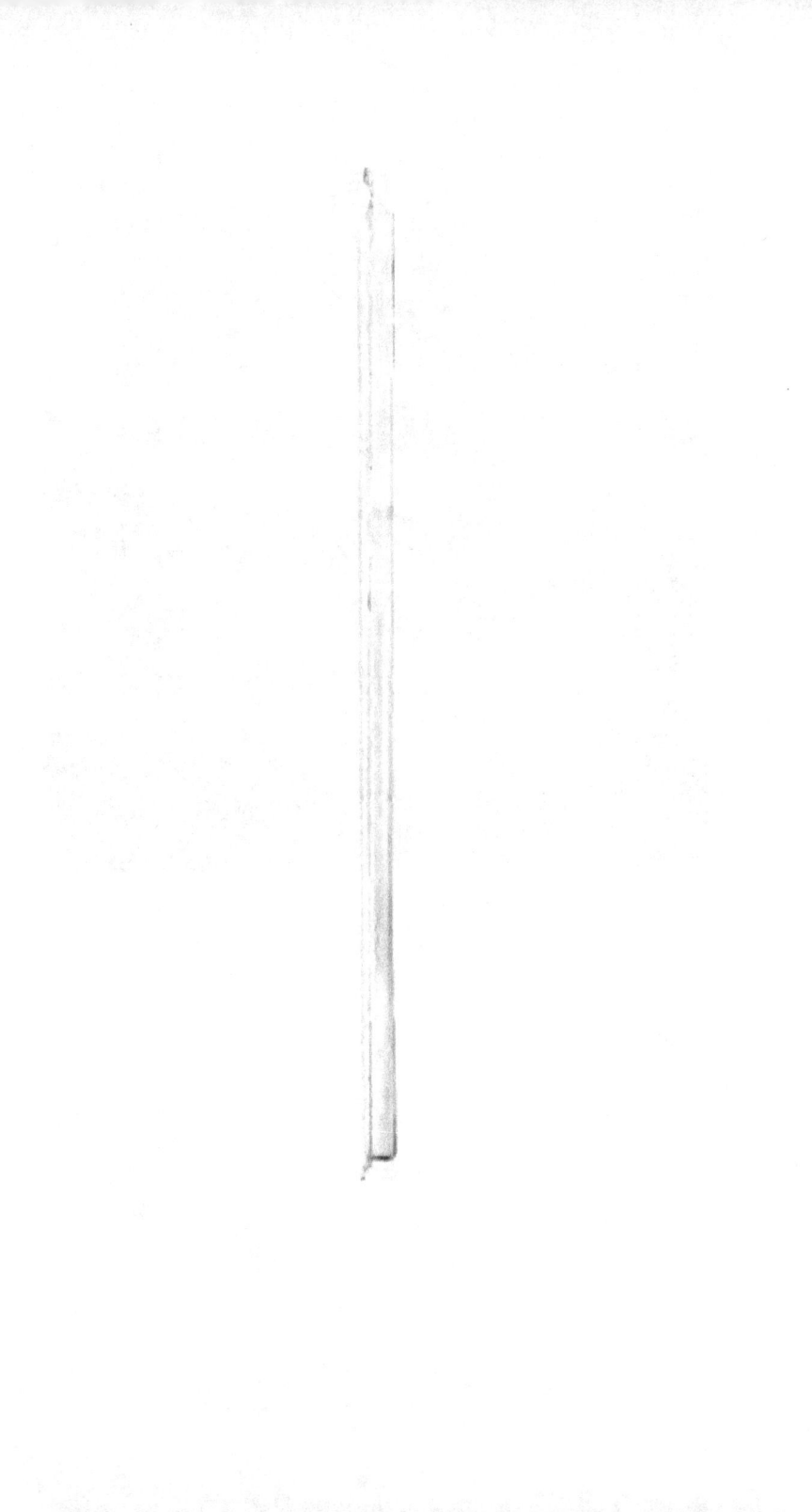

Wotton Hill.

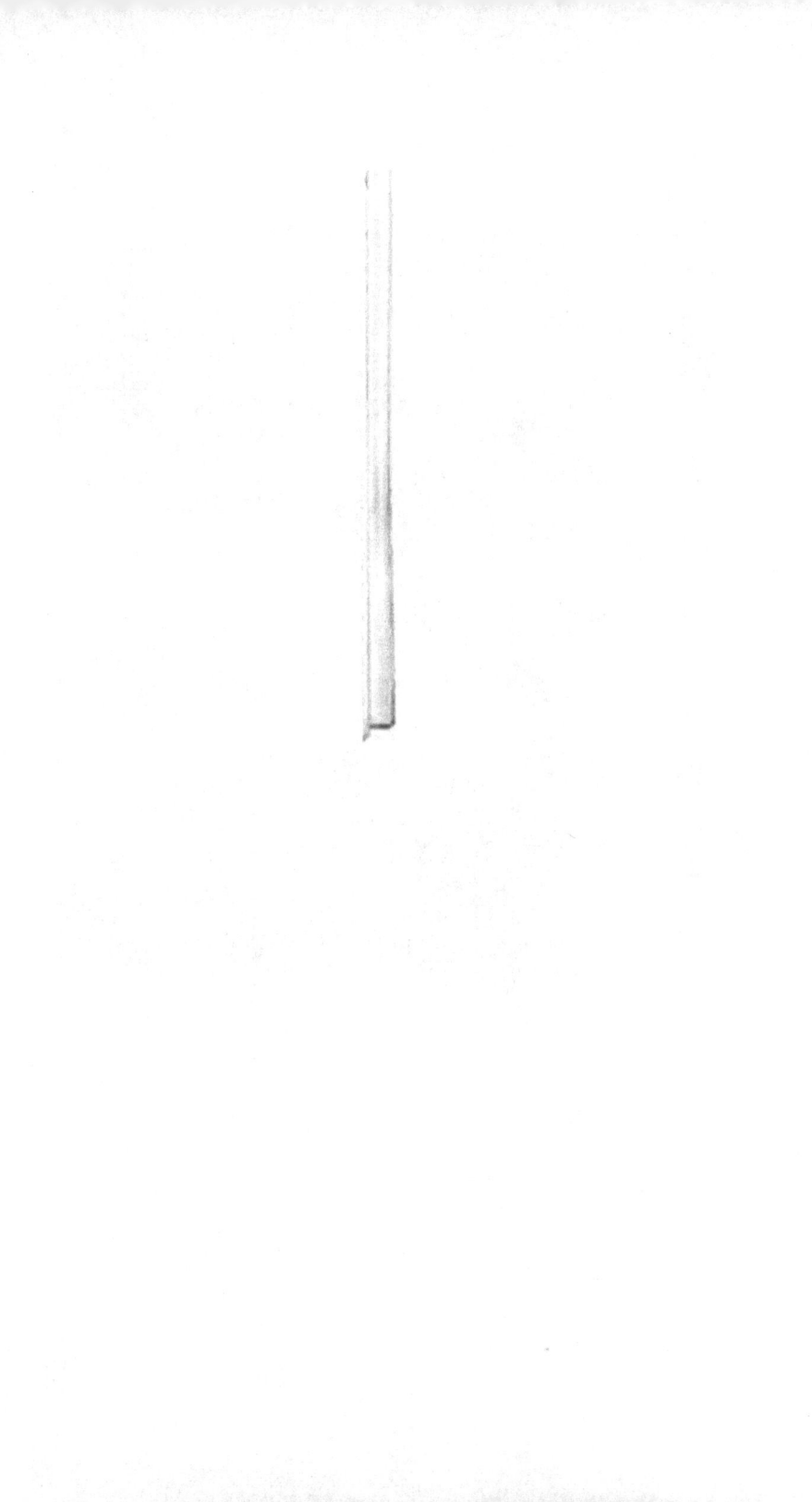

rish Church.

Ch

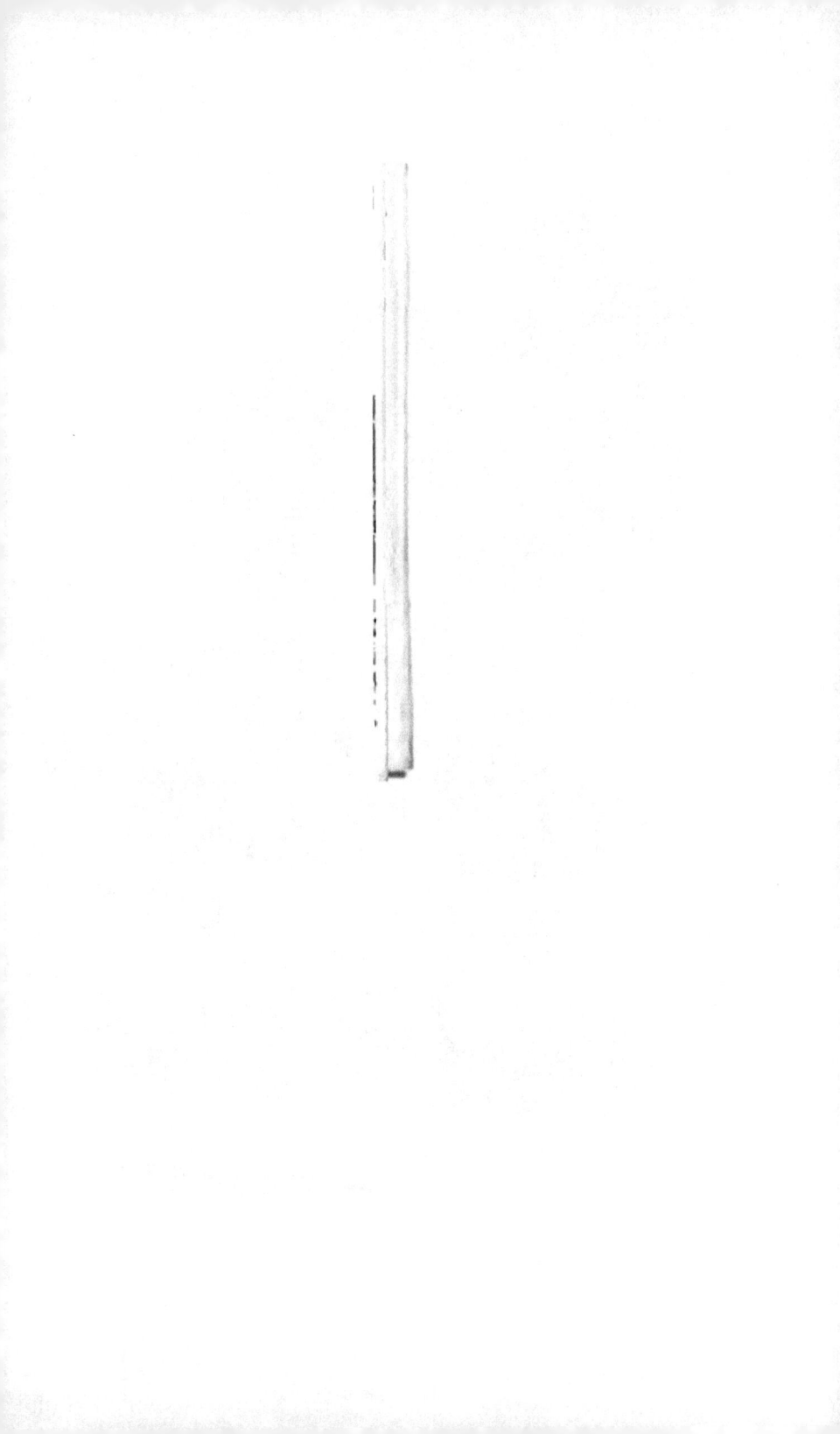

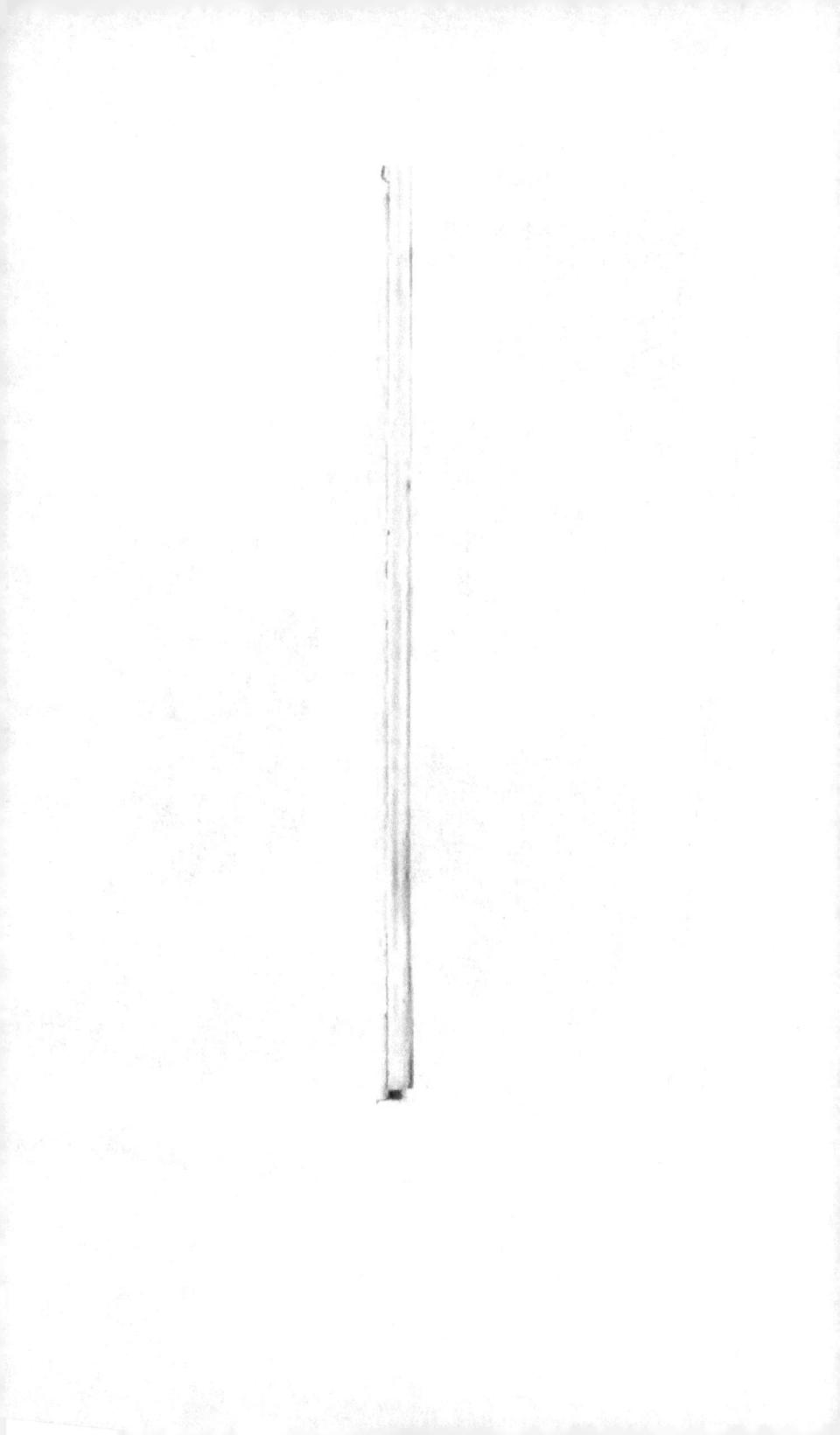

Old Town.

North Nibley Church.
North Nibley.

North Nibley.

Kingswood Abbey.

Tortworth Church.

Tortworth Church.

Tortworth Court

www.ingramcontent.com/pod-product-compliance
Lightning Source LLC
Chambersburg PA
CBHW021942160426
43195CB00011B/1196